CHANGING
THE
ABUSIVE
PARENT

Arnold P. Goldstein
Harold Keller   Diane Erné

RESEARCH PRESS

2612 North Mattis Avenue
Champaign, Illinois 61821

Advisory Editor, Frederick H. Kanfer

With our deepest gratitude to the parent aides of Alliance, creative pioneers in the use of Structured Learning with abusive parents:

Leola Brown
Darlene George
Lucy Kroft
Nancy Martin
Bernie McKeon
Joan McWain
Diane Morgan
Pat Riley
Carol Sawyer
Linda Simmons
Pat Stiles
Mary Jane Wood
Rose Ziverts

Contents

Acknowledgments

The Structured Learning approach to psychological skills training has a 15-year development history and, in its diverse applications, has benefitted greatly from the creative efforts of several persons. Robert Sprafkin and Jane Gershaw, in particular, helped launch and nurture this intervention approach, and thus their thinking and energy is very much reflected in the pages that follow. Its utilization with abusive parents has been greatly aided by several members of the Alliance staff. John Sweeney and John Warren, especially, have made several cogent "how-to" suggestions that are concretely reflected in many places throughout this book, thus adding substantially to its usefulness as an intervention guide.

The use of Structured Learning with abusive parents, though indeed resting on the foundation provided by those acknowledged above and the efforts of this book's authors, could not have gone forward without the creative, persevering, pioneering leadership of the parent aides of Alliance, to whom this book is so gratefully dedicated.

Introduction

This book seeks to accomplish two goals, to inform and to prepare. It describes in concrete detail an effective skills training approach to the reduction of physical abuse of children by their parents. The background, methods, and supporting research evidence for this approach are each presented. Thus, we seek to inform in the sense of developing a comprehensive understanding of this intervention; we seek to prepare in that a careful reading of the chapters that follow will be sufficient for most readers to be able to plan, organize, and actually conduct effective skills training groups.

The nature of child abuse, the diverse methods used for its remediation thus far, and the background of our approach are examined in depth in Chapters One, Two, and Three respectively. These three chapters will aid considerably the reader's goal of placing our skills training approach in an appropriate historical and contemporary context. Chapters Four through Eight are devoted to Structured Learning, our systematic means of teaching self-control, parenting, marital, and general interpersonal skills to abusive parents. These are largely "how-to" chapters, taking the reader step-by-step through the selection of trainers and assessment, selection, and grouping of abusive parents into potentially effective Structured Learning groups (Chapter Four), the Structured Learning training procedures (Chapter Five) and skill curriculum (Chapter Six), an illustrative transcript of a typical Structured Learning session (Chapter Seven), and the host of possible problems that may occur in such groups, as well as an array of techniques for reducing or eliminating their negative impact on trainee skill learning (Chapter Eight). Two final chapters complete our presentation. The first, involving the agency context, is written largely for administrators and seeks to provide a concrete illustration of how a particular child abuse agency came to heavily employ Structured Learning, problems that arose in this regard along the way, and our perceptions of its current functioning value in this agency today. Finally, we believe that all psychological interventions, ours included, must thrive or pass from the treatment scene based on their empirically demonstrated effectiveness or lack thereof. In our concluding chapter, we present an extended series of evaluative investigations, each of which sought to test, directly and comprehensively, the skill training potency of the Structured Learning approach.

It is our enduring hope that this book will aid in the broader implementation and use of Structured Learning with abusive parents and, consequently, will foster more constructive and skilled behaviors by such persons in their real world interactions with each other, with relatives and friends and, most especially, with their children.

Chapter One

Child Abuse: The Problem

Maltreatment of children by their parents and primary caregivers has been with us for a long time. Family violence can be traced back to ancient Rome and to both Old and New Testament biblical times (Exod. 1:16, 1:22; Matt. 2:16). Ross (1980) has documented a long history of child abuse from the sixteenth century to the present. Severe disciplinary practices based upon the view of children as parents' property and justified by biblical passages ("discipline for God") were the cultural norm. Indeed, even today, some abusive parents justify their actions through the quotation of biblical passages.

Cross-cultural anthropological studies show that child abuse is not limited to cultures with a Judeo-Christian heritage. Both primitive and advanced cultures of many types are reported to have engaged in extreme parental punitiveness of children (Korbin, 1977). Abusive treatment of children, therefore, is neither a recent phenomenon nor is it associated with a single cultural heritage.

Extreme parental punitiveness has been recognized as a serious problem that demands intervention only relatively recently. While several court cases in the United States in the nineteenth century dramatized the plight of abused children (interestingly, through actions of the Society for the Prevention of Cruelty to Animals) and established legal and social precedents for interventions on behalf of maltreated children, widespread public recognition of child abuse did not occur until 1962. In that year, Kempe and his research group published their medical article on the "battered child syndrome" (Kempe, Silverman, Steele, Droegenmueller, & Silver, 1962). That article resulted in broad media coverage of the problem and in the passage, under federal pressure, of laws for reporting child abuse in most states. Currently all states have such laws, and federal statutes result in the maintenance of child abuse records and the funding of demonstration projects and research on child maltreatment. The American Humane Association (AHA, 1981) indicates there has been a steady yearly increase from 1976 to 1981 in the number of reports of child abuse. Other countries have explicitly prohibited the use of corporal punishment of children and define child abuse broadly as part of general health services for children (Kahn & Kamerman, 1980). The growing recognition of and concern with the problem of child abuse is also reflected in the dozens of popular and professional books on the topic since the 1960s (see Keller & Erné, 1983, for a partial listing).

We will be examining child abuse in this book using a comprehensive model presented in detail by Keller and Erné (1983). This model requires a careful study of families at multiple levels, including the abusive parent, the child victim, patterns of parent-child interactions, the family context, and the community and broader social context in which the abuse takes place. This chapter presents a definition of child abuse, examines its incidence and consequences, and discusses several aspects of the comprehensive model.

It is important to note that the scope of this book is the physical abuse of children, not sexual or psychological abuse nor the problem of neglect. The change strategies presented in this book are focused primarily at physically abusive parents, although they have been used successfully with neglectful and sexually abusive parents as well. The following discussions of abuse will be limited to physical abuse.

DEFINITIONS OF CHILD ABUSE

There is no agreed upon definition of child abuse. Different definitions have been developed for various legal, clinical, social service, and research purposes. Even within these fields, there is a lack of consistency of definition. This often results in misleading and contradictory conclusions regarding the abusive parents, child victims, and intervention strategies and also leads to imprecise incidence reports.

For this book, we shall examine a number of definitions of physical abuse. There are three basic approaches to the definition of physical abuse and variations of each of these approaches (Alvy, 1975; Burgess, 1979; Gelles, 1975, 1980a, 1980b, 1982b; Gelles & Straus, 1979; Helfer, 1978; Keller & Erné, 1983; Parke & Collmer, 1975; Ross & Zigler, 1980; Straus, 1979a; Zigler, 1980). One approach is in terms of actions or outcomes. Straus (1979a) defined child abuse as "an attack by a parent involving punching, kicking, biting, hitting with an object, using a knife or gun" (p. 213). Such a focus upon action or outcome allows the abuse to be quantified with a minimum of inferences about the intent of the abusing parent. It has the disadvantage of not discriminating between accidental and intentional injuries.

A second approach to defining physical abuse specifically uses the concept of intention. Here child abuse involves a parental act carried out with the intent of physically hurting the child (Kempe & Helfer, 1972). Included within this definition are actions by a caregiver that result in "nonaccidental" harm to a child. Intent is not directly observable, so when using this definition we must infer it from the preceding conditions and the social context in which the injury occurred. As children's protective services workers know, reliably judging intent is difficult at best.

A third approach to defining child abuse incorporates both of the above definitions and also focuses on abuse as a culturally determined, or community defined, label (Parke & Collmer, 1975). This approach takes into account intentions, antecedents, the form and intensity of the actions, extent of injury, and the role and status of the perpetrator and victim before making a social judgment of actions that result in injury. This orientation has considerable appeal to us, and we will employ Parke and Collmer's definition of child abuse in this book. They define an abused youngster as "any child who receives non-accidental physical injury (or injuries) as a result of acts (or omissions) on the part of his parents or guardians that violate the community standards concerning the treatment of children" (p. 513).

INCIDENCE OF CHILD ABUSE

It is very difficult to determine the incidence of child abuse because of its varying definitions in the literature and across states. Further, the fact that child abuse is, in most instances, a private act that cannot be directly assessed also interferes considerably with accurate incidence data. The decision as to whether or not to label a family as abusive is typically based upon subjective professional judgment rather than on objective defining criteria. A further source of confusion, as Cohen and Sussman (1975) indicate, is that many states fail to distinguish between reports of abuse and of neglect. In addition, most states do not distinguish between number of reports of suspected abuse and neglect and number of confirmed cases.

National estimates of physical abuse range from Light's (1973) estimate of around 200,000 to 500,000 per year to Gil's (1970) estimate of 2.5 to 4.0 million cases per year. Data from the National Center on Child Neglect and Abuse show that almost 750,000 children were reported as abused or neglected (American Humane Association, 1981). This was a 15.7 percent increase in report rate over the previous year. The AHA report indicated that 40 percent of the individual abuse and neglect cases were confirmed, and that neglect reports outnumbered abuse reports in a 2:1 ratio.

An alternative approach to estimating the incidence of child abuse is to assess large samples of families concerning their use of violent child rearing practices. In perhaps the most comprehensive study of this type, Gelles (1978, 1980a, 1980b) interviewed a national sample of 1146 couples with children between the ages of 3 to 17 using the Conflict Tactics Scale (Straus, 1979b). Gelles found that 3.6 percent of the children from these families were at risk for serious injury through parental use of at least one dangerous form of violence—kicking, biting, hitting (beyond spanking), beating up, using a gun or knife—during 1975. Based upon census data for that year, this figure translates into 1.4 to 1.9 million children living with both parents being vulnerable to physical abuse in a year. It must be noted that while this survey was very careful and thorough, the figures are probably underestimates. The likelihood of underestimates may be due to a number of factors: parental self-reports provided the data (presumably parents wished to present themselves in socially desirable ways to an interviewer), only two-parent families were surveyed, the violent acts of only one of the two parents were recorded, and only children between the ages of 3 and 17 were included. At the same time, this study has been criticized for extrapolating national incidence figures for some forms of violence that occurred at an extremely low rate in the survey sample (Pelton, 1979).

Research on occurrence rate has reported that as many as half of the abused children in research samples have had previous abuse or are abused again (Ebbin, Gollub, Stein, & Wilson, 1969; Herrenkohl & Herrenkohl, 1979; Lauer, Broeck, & Grossman, 1974; Morse, Sahler, & Friedman, 1970; Simons, Downs, Hurster, & Archer, 1966). An examination of the records over a 10-year span of 286 families with verified child abuse found 67 percent had a second recorded abuse incident, and 54 percent of the families had two to five additional recorded incidents (Herrenkohl, Herrenkohl, Egolf, & Seech, 1979). Gelles' (1980a) national survey indicated that a single incident of a dangerous form of violence occurred in only 6 percent of the families studied. The average number of assaults on a child per year was 10.5 with a median of 4.5. The relatively high rate of recurrent abuse episodes indicates that the use of physical force within families is likely to be part of a general pattern of child rearing, rather than just a single isolated incident.

The types of injuries that abused children receive most frequently are a second category of incidence data. The most common injuries that abused children receive are bruises, abrasions, lacerations, and to a lesser extent burns and fractures (Gil, 1970). The "battered child syndrome," which is characterized by subdural hematoma, long bone fractures, and soft-tissue swelling, is suffered by a substantial percentage of abused children seen in hospital emergency rooms. For example, Simons et al. (1966) found this syndrome in 22 percent of a sample of 313 abuse cases from hospitals. The American Humane Association (1981) reports, however, that minor physical abuse occurs approximately 10 times more frequently than either major physical injury or burns.

DEMOGRAPHIC CHARACTERISTICS RELATED TO INCIDENCE OF CHILD ABUSE

Friedrich and Einbender (1983) have reviewed a number of demographic characteristics in relation to child abuse. Many of these characteristics create high levels of stress within the family. Whether or not such increased stress leads to child abuse will depend to some extent upon the stress coping skills of the individual family members as well as the contribution of the other persons who play a role in a comprehensive model of child abuse. Demographic characteristics that relate to child abuse will be summarized next.

Age of Child

Hospital based studies report that at least two-thirds of abused children are under 6 years of age (Simons et al., 1966; Zuckerman, Ambuel, & Bandman, 1972), with some studies indicating as many as 60 percent of abused children being less than 2 years old (Ebbin et al., 1969; Lauer et al., 1974). Bennie and Sclare (1969) and Kempe et al. (1962) found that children under 3 years of age were at the greatest risk of being abused.

At the same time, data from Gil (1970) and the American Humane Association (1981) show that child abuse is certainly not limited to preschool children and infants. They reported that 50–60 percent of the abused (and neglected) children in their samples were older than 6 years of age. Of Gil's sample of abused children, 20 percent were teenagers.

The AHA reported that major physical injuries (severe or fatal) occurred most frequently from birth to 3 years of age, decreased with increasing age, then increased during ages 12 through 16. Gelles' (1980a) survey showed a similar pattern. He found that the youngest (3 to 5 years of age) and oldest (15 to 17 years of age) groups in his sample were most vulnerable to physical abuse. Both the AHA and Gelles data thus show a "U-shaped" relationship between age and physical abuse. Gelles also reported that the oldest children in his survey were most likely to be victims of extreme forms of violence (beatings, guns, and knives).

The previously cited study on abuse reoccurrence rates (Herrenkohl et al., 1979) found that younger children were at greater risk than older children for experiencing recurrent abuse. This could be because younger children are less able than older ones to leave the family setting on their own (by running away, for example). Other possible explanations for the greater vulnerability of the younger children to abuse include their greater need for care and parental attention, thus potentially leading to more parental frustration, their lower ability to defend themselves or avoid physical punishment, and their greater fragility.

Sex of Child

Typically, no significant difference between the proportion of males and females who are victims of physical abuse has been reported (American Humane Association, 1981; Ebbin et al., 1969; Simons et al., 1966; Smith & Hanson, 1974). There may be some differences, though, when particular age groups are examined. Gil (1970) reported that below 12 years of age boys outnumbered girls as victims of abuse, but above 12 years, girls outnumbered boys (almost twice as many). The AHA reported a similar shift, though not quite as dramatic. Gelles' (1980a) survey found that boys were slightly more likely to be abused than girls throughout the 3 to 17 year age range.

Size of Family

Gelles (1980a) found that violence towards children varied with the size of the family. There was an inverted-U-shaped relationship between family size and child abuse. The abuse rate increased to a peak level for families with five children, then decreased with the lowest rate for families with eight or more children. Inadequate spacing of children is also related to child abuse (Hunter & Kilstrom, 1979; Hunter, Kilstrom, Kraybill, & Loda, 1978).

Abuse of One or More Children in Family

Parke and Collmer (1975) have suggested that abuse sometimes represents a scapegoating of one child within a family unit. Gil (1970), however, noted that abuse of more than one child occurred in about 30 percent of the families in his study. Herrenkohl et al. (1979) reported that half of their studied families had more than one target of abuse.

It should be noted that even when more than one child is not abused in a family with multiple children, siblings of an abused child may develop very negative attitudes towards their parents. Halperin (1981) found that both abused children and their nonabused siblings had much more negative perceptions of their family members than children from nonabusive families.

Racial or Ethnic Background of Family

Some statistics suggest that nonwhite children are more likely to be abused than white children (American Humane Association, 1981; Gil, 1970; Thomson, Paget, Bates, Mesch, & Putnam, 1971). Other investigators have not found racial or ethnic group differences (Billingsley, 1969; Elmer, 1977; Gelles, 1980a; Young, 1964). Those differences that have been found may be due to ethnic differences in child rearing practices, biases in reporting practices, and the greater prevalence of lower socioeconomic conditions among nonwhites.

Socioeconomic Status of Family

Child abuse occurs across socioeconomic levels. However, children from lower socioeconomic status families are much more likely to be victims of abuse (Gelles, 1980a; Giovannoni & Billingsley, 1970; Pelton, 1978; Smith, Hanson, & Noble, 1975; Steinberg, Catalano, & Dooley, 1981; Straus, 1979a). Gelles has shown that this reported relationship between socioeconomic status and abuse exists for various indices of status, including education, income, occupation, and unemployment or underemployment.

Both Gelles and Pelton have argued persuasively that the most important factor in the relationship between socioeconomic status and abuse is the presence of multiple stresses experienced by poor and low socioeconomic status families. The previously reported relationship between family size and abuse rate varies with socioeconomic status (Gelles, 1980a). Among the poorest families, each additional child increased the likelihood of child abuse. In middle income families, the abuse rate increased with each child up to seven, but not beyond this number. There was no relationship between number of children and abuse rate for wealthy families.

Number of Parents in Family

Research has also shown that 30-42 percent of abused children come from single-parent households (American Humane Association, 1981; Gil, 1970; Maden & Wrench, 1977; Zigler, 1980). Such an abuse rate is disproportionate to the number of single-parent families in the country. Again, one could argue that stress within such households might be a critical factor in the abuse rate. It has also been shown that children who are living with one natural parent and one stepparent are more likely to become victims of abuse (Daly & Wilson, 1980; Hunter et al., 1978).

Other Child Characteristics

Numerous theoretical presentations and reviews of the abuse literature suggest additional child characteristics that increase the likelihood of abuse (Belsky, 1978; Friedrich & Boriskin, 1976, 1978; Garbarino, 1977; Gil, 1970; Green, Gaines, & Sandgrund, 1974; Rose & Hardman, 1981; Sameroff & Chandler, 1975). These characteristics include being disabled or handicapped, difficult (e.g., colicky or hyperactive), of the "wrong" sex, and of low birth weight and premature. In a prospective study (i.e., monitoring families across time from before the child's birth onward), Hunter and Kilstrom (1979) and Hunter et al. (1978) found that abusing parents had the most seriously impaired newborns. Nonabusing parents (through a followup of 1 year after birth) had relatively healthier infants who were larger at birth, had fewer defects or residual medical problems, were 1 month closer to term, and behaved more like normal newborns. Similarly, Sherrod, O'Connor, Vietze, and Altemeier (1984) studied the hospital records (both inpatient and outpatient) of abused, neglected, and nonabused children over the first 3 years of life. They found that children from abusive families (both abuse victims and nonabused siblings) were ill more often than nonabused children, particularly during the first few months after birth before abuse had been reported. Such difficult children are likely to increase stress in families, thus increasing the possibility of abuse in a parent lacking parenting skills or having difficulty controlling anger.

CONSEQUENCES OF CHILD ABUSE

There are a number of problems with much of the research on the consequences of abuse for the victim. Until recently, there were no studies that included control groups to determine whether the frequency or magnitude of identified problems was any different from that found in samples of nonabused children of comparable backgrounds. Kinard (1980) indicated additionally that early studies used small and select samples of abused children and, especially in research on emotional consequences, poor measurement instruments. It is not clear, except in prospective research, whether problems observed in an abused sample (even if different from those of a control group) are due to the abuse or whether the problems existed prior to the abuse.

In spite of the problems with research, it is apparent that the harmful effects of child abuse range from superficial wounds to permanent neurological, intellectual and cognitive, and behavioral, emotional, and personality impairment. Research on each of these areas will be reviewed next in this section. And we will also discuss the most consistent and insidious finding in the child abuse literature—the fact that abusing parents often were themselves physically or emotionally abused or neglected as children.

Neurological Consequences

Research on neurological consequences in abused children illustrates the problem of determining whether symptoms precede the abuse or occur as a result of it (Sandgrund, Gaines, & Green, 1974). Almost all data in this area come from case studies and retrospective screening of hospital records (i.e., examination of prior records after the abuse occurs). Case studies have reported chronic subdural hematomas, possible retardation, microcephaly, and diffuse and nonfocal neurological signs that appear to result from abuse including shaking of infants (leading to whiplash) and rough handling (Baron, Bejar, & Sheaff, 1970; Caffey, 1972; Oliver, 1975).

In a 5-year follow-up study of 58 abused children, Martin, Beezley, Conway, and Kempe (1974) found that 53 percent of the children had some neurological abnormalities. Of those, 31 percent of the children had some neurological dysfunction, thus seriously handicapping their everyday functioning. It is important to note that these children, as well as another abused sample (Green, Voeller, Gaines, & Kubie, 1981), had neurological abnormalities even without a history of head trauma.

Intellectual and Cognitive Consequences

Clinically, it is generally assumed that physical abuse results in lowered intelligence (Lynch, 1978) and delays in language development (Blager & Martin, 1976). Clinical research with no comparison groups of nonabused samples has reported that between 26 and 57 percent of the abused samples were considered mentally retarded and/or placed in special classes for retarded children (Elmer & Gregg, 1967; Hyman & Mitchell, 1975; Kline, 1977; Martin, 1972; Martin et al., 1974; Morse et al., 1970). Review of hospital records indicates that 3 to 10 percent of mental retardation in children may have been caused by abuse (Buchanan & Oliver, 1977).

Control group studies with infants and toddlers are highly supportive of the conclusion that abuse is related to intellectual and cognitive deficits. While retardation is not always observed with abused children in these studies, the maltreated children are consistently and significantly found to have lower scores on measures of intellectual and cognitive functioning (Appelbaum, 1977; Dietrich, Starr, & Kaplan, 1980; Fitch, Cadol, Goldson, Wendell, Swartz, & Jackson, 1976; Gregg & Elmer, 1969; Koski & Ingram, 1977). Controlled studies with preschoolers (Fitch et al., 1976; Friedrich, Einbender, & Luecke, 1983; Perry, Doran, & Wells, 1983) and with elementary-school-aged children (Barahal, Waterman, & Martin, 1981; Perry et al., 1983) have shown similar, though less dramatic, significant differences in intelligence test scores. Perry et al. (1983) compared an emotionally disturbed sample of abused children with a control group and found there were significant language skill deficits among the abused children.

Elmer's (1977, 1978) 8-year follow-up studies with a sample of abused children and a control group of accidentally injured low income children found numerous developmental problems in both groups and no differences in intellectual functioning. Elmer suggested that abuse by itself is not the critical factor in these developmental deficits. Rather she suggested that the primary factor is the pervasive and stressful consequences of an impoverished environment. Starr's (1982) control group research with abused and nonabused low income children supported this conclusion when no differences were found on measures of cognitive functioning. However, the potential role of abuse in intellectual deficits is strongly suggested in the control group study of Barahal et al. (1981) where significant impairments in intellectual functioning for abused school-aged children who were not from economically disadvantaged families were found. In addition, there was no neurological impairment in their sample of abused children.

Clearly, with respect to the intellectual and cognitive consequences of child abuse, it is important to examine children prospectively and to examine abused children across time to determine whether differences persist with time. It is also important to try to separate the effects of abuse from other pervasive conditions in a child's life.

Behavioral, Emotional, and Personality Consequences

Behaviorally, abused children have been described as either very passive and withdrawn or very active and aggressive (Martin & Beezley, 1976; Mirandy, 1976). Martin and Beezley (1977) conducted a thorough study with abused children (though without a control group) that led them to characterize such children as having an impaired ability to enjoy life (apparently due to ineffective and anxious efforts to please others), psychiatric symptoms (such as enuresis, tantrums, hyperactivity, and bizarre behavior), low self-esteem, school learning problems, social withdrawal, oppositional behavior, hypervigilance to adult cues, compulsivity, and pseudoadult behavior. Similar patterns of behavior were described by Kline (1977).

Abuse may also vary with criminal or deviant behavior. Mac-Keith (1975) cited studies in Germany where a large proportion of criminals and murderers had been maltreated in childhood. Similarly, a large majority of delinquent and socially deviant adolescents in the United States indicate they were abused as children (Alfaro, 1978; Helfer & Kempe, 1976; Lewis, Shanok, Pincus, & Glaser, 1979; Steele, 1976b). Baer and Wathey (1977) reported a high incidence of abuse in the history of young adult drug abusers.

In control group studies, abused children have been found to be more aggressive than nonabused comparison youngsters (Green, 1978a; Kinard, 1980; Reidy, 1977). The severity of abuse was directly related to the amount of aggression shown on psychological tests (Kinard, 1982). Physically abused children were also found to be significantly more self-destructive, evidencing more suicide attempts and self-mutilation (Green, 1978b). A similar relationship between abuse and self-mutilation was found by Carroll, Schaffer, Spensley, and Abramowitz (1980).

Barahal et al. (1981) compared what they called social-cognitive styles of abused and nonabused children. They found that abused children had little confidence in their ability to influence their own experiences. In particular, they felt that negative outcomes were beyond their own personal control. The abused children were also less able to understand subtle and complex interpersonal relationships. Abused and control children did not differ in their moral judgments. Straker and Jacobson (1981) found that school-aged abused children were less empathic and were more socially maladjusted. Kinard (1980) also found lower emotional functioning among abused children. The abused children were more likely to misperceive trust situations than nonabused children. Perry et al. (1983), in a study with abused and nonabused preschool and school-aged children, found that mothers reported the abused children to have more abnormal behaviors and poorer self- and school-adjustment.

While there is no single behavioral style that is characteristic of abused children, the presence of socioemotional problems in many maltreated children is well documented. The consequences of the abuse will vary with the developmental level of the child, the duration and intensity of abuse, and the quality of the subsequent home environment and community support.

The Intergenerational Abuse Cycle

As indicated earlier, the most consistent and insidious finding in the child abuse literature is that abusing parents often report having been physically or emotionally abused or neglected themselves as children. The finding that abusive parents raise their children in the manner in which they themselves were raised has been obtained in numerous studies (Fontana, 1968; Justice & Justice, 1976; Kempe & Helfer, 1972; Kempe et al., 1962; Lukianowicz, 1971; Lystad, 1975; Melnick & Hurley, 1969; Oliver & Taylor, 1971; Ounsted, Oppenheimer, & Lindsay, 1975; Sameroff & Chandler, 1975; Silver, Dublin, & Lourie, 1969; J. Smith & Rachman, 1984; S. Smith & Hanson, 1975; Spinetta & Rigler, 1972; Steele, 1976a, 1976b; Steele & Pollock, 1968). While each of these studies was conducted with a relatively select sample, this same finding was obtained by Gelles (1980a) in his national survey. Further, the abuse rate in the national sample was higher for those parents who had experienced abuse at least twice a year as teenagers as compared to those who had experienced abuse once a year or not at all as teenagers. Gelles also found that merely observing violence in the home as a child was an important factor in abusive behavior; that is, those individuals who reported that they had witnessed their parents hit one another or another sibling had a much higher violence rate toward their own children than people who indicated they had never seen their parents do that. In a retrospective control group study, Conger, Burgess, and Barrett (1979) found a significantly greater history of punitive child rearing among abusive parents than among a control group of parents.

Some writers in the popular media and professional literature suggest that *if* individuals are abused as children *then* they will become child abusers as parents. Such a statement is an overgeneralization. Certainly that is a likely consequence of abuse for a given individual. But it is important to note that the fact that many abusive parents report having been abused as children does not mean that children who are abused will necessarily grow up to be abusive parents. There are individuals who have not been abused as child-en who become abusive, as well as individuals who have been abused and do not subsequently abuse their own children.

The following studies indicate why abuse may or may not be transmitted across generations. Hunter et al. (1978) conducted a 1-year prospective study of 255 infants and their families. They searched the state registry for confirmed reports of abuse 1 year after the study ended and found 10 (3.9 percent). That percentage is comparable to the percentage found in Gelles' (1980a) national survey. Of the 10 abused children, 9 came from families with a parental history of an abusive and neglectful childhood. Hunter and Kilstrom (1979) made an intensive study of the files of those 9 families and compared them with 40 families from the Hunter et al. (1978) study who had a similar history of the parents having been abused as children. The infants in those 40 families were not reported as maltreated in that same 1-year period. At least for the 1-year period involved in this study, this set of 40 families broke out of the apparent family pattern of transmitting a cycle of abusive parenting across generations. The investigators found that the 40 nonabusive families had a broader network of available resources and different family interactional patterns than the abusive families. That is, the nonabusive families were more likely to have available to them friends or an extended family, were more likely to participate in religious or other social groups, and were more skilled at using the services of community agencies.

This highlights an important set of skills that at least partially can break the intergenerational cycle of abuse. It also suggests other levels that need to be considered within Keller and Erné's (1983) model of child abuse. Thus far we have concentrated primarily on the child victim. We turn now to a fuller consideration of other components of the comprehensive model.

THE ABUSING PARENT

Research concerned with the characteristics, particularly personality characteristics, of abusive parents is based largely upon case records or personal interviews with single cases or small, nonrandom, clinical samples (for reviews see Cicchetti, Taraldson, & Egeland, 1978; Isaacs, 1981; Keller & Erné, 1983; Lystad, 1975; Parke & Collmer, 1975; Sameroff & Chandler, 1975; Spinetta & Rigler, 1972). Studies with control groups of nonabusing parents are rare (the Melnick & Hurley, 1969, study being an early exception). No consistent set of personality characteristics has been identified. Personality traits, especially in early studies, are identified by clinical judgments. Few studies use sound measures. Even with control groups, sample and measurement differences make comparison across studies difficult.

Writers in the child abuse literature initially suggested the presence of psychoses as a major contributing factor in child abuse. However, Spinetta and Rigler (1972), in a review of personality characteristics of abusive parents, indicated that later studies showed that less than 10 percent of abusing parents showed severe psychotic tendencies. Kempe and Kempe (1976) found that only 10 to 15 percent of their abusing parents had extremely poor prognoses for change. That small percentage included individuals classified as psychotics, those having severe character disorders (e.g., extreme alcoholism and drug addiction), and "fanatics" (e.g., persons with extreme religious beliefs, unusual philosophies of life, or extreme moralism).

Keller and Erné (1983) reviewed and presented numerous demographic and personality characteristics, as well as skill deficits, that have been related to abusive parents. Some of these have already been indicated earlier in the chapter, such as having been abused oneself, large family size and close spacing of children, single parenting, low socioeconomic status, and lack of education. Other characteristics that they found related to abuse include early parenthood, sex of parent (with females generally being more likely to be the abusive parent), and low intelligence. All of these factors relate to the likelihood of greater stress and the greater demands upon individual parent's skills in dealing with the stresses accompanying these factors. For example, the fact that females are more frequently abusers than males is often attributed to their spending more time with the children and to their being more likely to be blamed for the children's misdeeds.

Personality characteristics of abusive parents that were listed by Keller and Erné included low self-esteem or self-concept, low intelligence, impulsivity, hostility, isolation and loneliness, anxiety, depression, rigidity, fear of rejection, being rejected, low frustration tolerance, role reversal (where the parent needs nurturance from the children), self-centeredness, fearfulness, immaturity and dependency, distrustfulness, neuroticism, abnormality, drug or alcohol abuse, and being criminal. Some investigators have attempted to identify clusters of personality characteristics for abusive parents (Delsordo, 1973; Merrill, 1962; Zalba, 1966, 1967). No consistent set of personality traits or clusters of personality traits have been identified as characterizing abusive parents.

A variety of skill, knowledge, and attitudinal deficits has also been suggested as characteristic of abusive parents (Keller & Erné, 1983). These deficits are found in parenting skills (including overuse of physical punishment), coping skills, self-control skills, marital skills, general interpersonal skills, and knowledge of child development (resulting in inappropriate expectations). Abusive parents are also characterized by negative child rearing attitudes, inability to distinguish feelings of self and others (particularly the child), and inaccurate attributions about intent or personal responsibility for one's own actions. These deficits and characteristics require further research to fully describe their role in the phenomenon of child abuse.

These skill deficits, we propose, appear to be particularly amenable to change strategies like that described in this book. Several types of skill deficits are shown by abusive parents within the context of their interactions with their children, as well as in the family and broader community contexts. These concerns are the focus of the last two sections of this chapter.

PARENT-CHILD INTERACTIONS

Research has shown a strong relationship between parent-child interactional patterns and abusive behavior (Burgess, 1979; Burgess & Conger, 1978; Conger, 1982). Burgess and Conger directly observed daily interactions of abusive, neglectful, and control families. The abusive and neglectful parents had lower overall rates of interaction, lower rates of positive interaction, and higher rates of negative interaction. The abusive mothers were the most different from the controls. Similarly, Egeland and Brunnquell (1979) found that abusive mothers displayed fewer appropriate caregiving behaviors and less positive affect during observations of abusive and nonabusive mothers. Abusive parents were observed to use ineffective and inconsistent punishment and discipline, including high levels of physical punishment, demands, and threats (Kimball, Stewart, Conger, & Burgess, 1980; Reid, Taplin, & Lorber, 1981).

Research on attachment or bonding (or the development of love between parent and child) has demonstrated the importance of early parent-child interactions within the first days of life, particularly with premature and ill newborns. In their previously cited prospective studies, Hunter and Kilstrom (1979) and Hunter et al. (1978) found that less parent-infant contact during early hospitalization was more likely to lead to abuse. In their study comparing families who did and did not break the intergenerational cycle of abuse, they found that families who broke the cycle visited their ill newborns soon after birth and much more often than the abusive families. Daly and Wilson (1980) cite a dramatic unpublished study by O'Connor and her associates in Nashville in which low income mothers (with their firstborn children) were randomly assigned to a hospital routine condition or an experimental condition allowing an additional 6 hours of mother-infant contact on each of the first 2 days after birth. In a 2-year follow-up, 9 of 143 children assigned to the hospital routine were victims of abuse, neglect, abandonment, or nonorganic failure to thrive in comparison with none of 134 children assigned to the experimental routine. This represents a highly significant reduction in risk based upon 12 extra hours of contact in the first 2 days of life. In a related finding Lynch (1975) found that 40 percent of a sample of severely abused children had been separated from their mothers during the first 48 hours after birth as opposed to 6 percent of their nonabused siblings.

Certainly parent-child interaction involves at least two participants. Many of the studies on interaction patterns fail to look at the behaviors of the child within these interactions. Those that have examined child behaviors point to the possible role of the child in eliciting stress and/or abusive behavior. For example, in a control group study, Wasserman, Green, and Allen (1983) observed that abusive mothers were more negative and less positive. At the same time the abused infants were observed to comply less with their mothers' attempts to direct their play during the observational sessions. Similarly, abused children were observed to display significantly more negative behavior than nonabused children in a family setting (Kimball et al., 1980). The overall rate of negative child behavior was greater in single-parent families than in two-parent families. The rate of negative behavior by children was related to the rate of negative behavior by parents in this latter study.

Treatment focused upon behaviors and skills relevant to these interactional patterns should have an effect upon the parent-child interactions and thus on abusive behaviors. In particular, training focusing upon parenting skills, communications skills, negotiation skills, and anger control should be beneficial. Research in this area of parent-child interactions needs to examine the mutual effects of each participant on the other participants within the interactions. Not only are parents influencing their children, but the children influence the parents' behavior as well. The effectiveness of interventions needs to be examined in relation to this mutual influence.

FAMILY, COMMUNITY, AND BROADER SOCIAL CONTEXTS

Garbarino (1977) has presented a theory of child abuse which describes the influence of various social contexts on the abuse problem. These social contexts include the family and community, as well as pervasive national and cultural values that are implicitly or explicitly communicated by social institutions and the media. Some research findings on these theoretically relevant contexts are described in this section.

Within the family context, abusive families are characterized as having marital conflicts, unsatisfactory marriages, and general family violence including verbal abuse (Alexander, 1972; Helfer, 1973; Hunter et al., 1978; Hyman, 1978; Lukianowicz, 1971; Milner & Wimberley, 1979, 1980; Ounsted et al., 1975; Straus, 1979a). Greater amounts of family stress and life changes, frequently associated with lower socioeconomic status families, are directly related to child abuse (Conger et al., 1979; Gaines, Sandgrund, Green, & Power, 1978; Gelles, 1980a; Giovannoni & Billingsley, 1970; Justice & Duncan, 1976). Families who share child care and decision making inequitably also have higher abuse rates (Gelles, 1980a, 1982a).

In addition to isolation within the family, abusive families are also often isolated from extended family, neighbors, and the broader community. Abusive families participate less in community organizations and make less use of available economic, health, and social resources. Giovannoni and Billingsley (1970) found that abusing mothers had less knowledge about community resources than a control group. Hunter et al. (1978) found that social isolation without adequate family support systems (both inside and outside the family context), poor use of medical services, and inadequate child care arrangements were all important factors related to abuse in their prospective study of families with premature and ill newborns.

These same factors (support of friends, neighbors, or extended family, participation in community organizations, and use of community agency services) were most important in breaking the intergenerational cycle of abuse (Hunter & Kilstrom, 1979). While not a control group study, Ayoub and Pfeifer (Ayoub & Pfeifer, 1977; Pfeifer & Ayoub, 1976) found that 85 percent of high risk families who refused help designed to reduce social isolation had their children removed from their homes on grounds of abuse or neglect within 6 to 12 months after initial identification. In comparison, none of the families who accepted the comprehensive programming had children reported or hospitalized for abuse or neglect over the same period of time.

Other studies have also suggested the importance of support, involvement in organizations, and use of community services in reducing child abuse. Straus (1979a) suggested that the lack of differences in abuse rate found among black and white families in Gelles (1978) national survey in spite of the generally lower socioeconomic status of the black families might have been due to the greater support provided by the extended black families. Egeland and Sroufe (1981a, 1981b) found improvement in mother-child attachment over time for those mothers in their prospective study who increased their social support network. Garbarino, Crouter, and Sherman (1977) suggested that the presence or absence of neighborhood economic and social resources (identified through the use of census tract data) accounted for neighborhood differences in abuse rates.

In an experimental test of the importance of community resources, Gray, Cutler, Dean, and Kempe (1976) (cited in Garbarino, 1977) identified 100 "abuse-prone" families. Fifty families were randomly assigned to supplementary services (an active visiting nurse who attempted to establish an enduring relationship with the family), and fifty families were randomly assigned to a control group receiving the typical community services. After 2 years, the control families had a significantly higher abuse rate, and no known abuse occurred in the experimental group.

Some writers have argued persuasively that child abuse is influenced by factors at broader institutional and national levels. These influences include the general acceptance of: the use of physical punishment (N. Feshbach, 1980; S. Feshbach, 1980; Garbarino, 1977; Gelles, 1980a, 1980b, 1982a; Gil, 1970; Steinmetz & Straus, 1974; Zigler, 1980), TV and magazine coverage of abuse (Gerbner, 1980; Signorielli, 1980), institutional abuse of children and handicapped people (Blatt, 1980; N. Feshbach, 1980), the use of corporal punishment of children in our schools (N. Feshbach, 1980), and an attitude of exploitation of the weak by the powerful (Albee, 1980). In other countries, laws prohibiting the corporal punishment of children may reduce the acceptance of violence against children (Kahn & Kamerman, 1980).

Intervention at these broader levels of influence is difficult but no less necessary. At the level of the family, skill enhancement techniques again are useful. Specifically, marital and communication skills should help with conflict and with intra- and extrafamily isolation. The previously cited research demonstrated the importance of isolation from potent resources as a critical factor in child abuse. However, even if resources are available, families need the knowledge and skills to make use of those resources. In addition, skills for coping with stress generally, and particularly with those stresses associated with lower socioeconomic status, are necessary treatment components. Negotiation skills and shared decision making will be important within many abusive families, as will the teaching of alternatives to verbal abuse and punishment, and the teaching of positive non-aversive styles of interaction.

Chapter Two

Child Abuse:
Intervention Approaches

Intervention approaches are related to the theoretical frameworks used in understanding child abuse. Numerous reviewers of the child abuse literature have grouped the various theoretical models into three general categories—psychiatric or intraindividual, sociological, and social situational (Burgess, 1979; Cicchetti et al., 1978; Gelles & Straus, 1979; Justice & Justice, 1976; Keller & Erné, 1983; Parke & Collmer, 1975). Each of these theoretical frameworks relates to one or more aspects of the comprehensive model of child abuse presented in the last chapter (Keller & Erné, 1983). In this chapter, we will review each of these theoretical models and the treatment strategies derived from them.

PSYCHIATRIC OR INTRAINDIVIDUAL MODEL

In this model, the abusing parent is viewed as the major cause of child abuse and thus is the primary focus of treatment. The psychiatric or intraindividual model (also referred to as the psychopathic, psychodynamic, personality or character trait, or mental illness model), assumes that abusive parents have certain personality characteristics that separate them from other parents. This model suggests that the abuser is mentally ill and therefore requires traditional psychodynamic verbal psychotherapy for change.

Studies of the causes of child abuse within this psychiatric perspective have focused primarily on the personality characteristics of the abuser. Initially it was suggested that the presence of psychoses was a major causal factor in child abuse. Evidence has not supported this, except for a very small minority of abuse cases (Keller & Erné, 1983; Kempe & Kempe, 1976; Spinetta & Rigler, 1972). As indicated in the previous chapter, no consistent set or clusters of personality traits have been identified as characterizing abusive parents. The major limitation of this perspective is the inadequate evidence showing personality characteristics of abusive parents to be the primary causal agents of child abuse. Critical reviews of the research methods and of the evidence for this position have been presented by numerous authors (Cicchetti et al., 1978; Isaacs, 1981; Keller & Erné, 1983; Lystad, 1975; Parke & Collmer, 1975; Sameroff & Chandler, 1975; Spinetta & Rigler, 1972).

Child abuse, as suggested in the previous chapter, is a complex phenomenon. We need to move away from conceptualizing child abuse as a homogeneous, unitary problem (Green et al., 1974; Lystad, 1975). Personality attributes of abusive parents, even if found consistently with further research, do not seem to be sufficient to cause child abuse in the absence of other predisposing factors within the family and larger social system. Descriptive information about abusive parents might be a useful starting point in understanding child abuse, but such information cannot provide a comprehensive explanation. Data do not allow adequate prediction of actual abusive behavior on the basis of parent characteristics (without additional information on other important factors), but knowledge of parent characteristics might be helpful in at least two other ways. First, such knowledge may be helpful in predicting parents at risk (Gray et al., 1976; Schneider, Helfer, & Pollock, 1972; Schneider, Hoffmeister, & Helfer, 1976; Schneider, Pollock, & Helfer, 1972). Creative intervention programs could then be offered to these parents. Second, research could attempt to relate parent characteristics to contextual variables and to different treatment strategies. Such research would help to identify what treatment strategies are best suited for what kinds of abusing parents in what kinds of situations. This is called prescriptive therapy (Goldstein, 1978; Goldstein & Stein, 1976).

The most common form of treatment in the psychiatric model has been individual psychoanalytically oriented psychotherapy. Such therapy, when used by skilled, experienced therapists, has been shown to be effective in some cases (Fontana, 1971; Steele, 1975), but long-term effectiveness has not been demonstrated. Individual analytic therapy is most successful when used with other treatment approaches, such as home observation and direct teaching of child rearing skills, knowledge, and attitudes (Steele, 1975). Resolution of psychological conflict with some emotional insight and understanding is typically considered important for permanent gains and for changing long-term emotional relationships. However, as Beezley, Martin, and Alexander (1976) point out, intellectual understanding without learning (or relearning) skills results in parents who can explain why and how they interact but who have changed nothing in their actual interactions.

Psychoanalytic treatment is a highly verbal, abstract, costly, and time consuming approach to change. Several factors, including personality characteristics, the disproportionate number of low socioeconomic status abusers, the lifestyle of abusive parents, intellectual deficits of many abusers, therapist time, client time, and monetary issues make such an approach impractical (Cicchetti et al., 1978; Kempe & Helfer, 1972; Parke & Collmer, 1975; Steele, 1975). Abusing parents may need more than a designated hour each week in order to refrain from abusing their children.

The theoretical, research, and treatment literature suggests that this model is very limited in its potential for bringing about lasting change in the abuse problem. Therefore, many researchers have suggested moving away from or beyond the psychiatric model of abuse to consider broader interpersonal and social contextual factors (Antler, 1978; Beezley et al., 1976; Gelles, 1975; Newberger & Bourne, 1978; Ross & Zigler, 1980).

SOCIOLOGICAL MODEL

The sociological model of abuse focuses on cumulative environmental stresses. Gil (1970) was perhaps the earliest proponent of this framework and of related social reforms derived from the approach. Emphasis is placed upon the role of cultural attitudes toward violence, social class and social stress factors, and family-community relationships that relate to social isolation. Variations of this model suggest that violence is used as a resource when other resources are lacking in relatively powerless families (Gelles & Straus, 1979).

Until recently, research supporting this model and interventions derived from it have been limited. Much of the research has been descriptive and correlational (not allowing a clear understanding of causal factors), with limited samples of abusing families. One issue that has received considerable attention concerns the relationship between socioeconomic status and child abuse. It is frequently argued that child abuse is classless, that it occurs at all socioeconomic levels. While it is quite accurate to say that child abuse does occur at all social levels (Gelles, 1980a, 1980b; Straus, 1979a), that does not mean there is no relationship between socioeconomic status and child abuse. Those who argue against a relationship between social class and child abuse suggest that associating the two further stigmatizes the lower class.

The middle and upper classes are probably disproportionately represented in unreported cases of child abuse. If those classes were more open to public scrutiny, more child abuse would be reported in them. Pelton (1978) suggests that "undiscovered evidence is not evidence." He believes that the public scrutiny argument does not explain why increased public awareness has not changed socioeconomic patterns of abuse, why child abuse is related to degrees of poverty within the lower socioeconomic levels, and why the most severe injuries occur within the poorest families. It must be noted that to say abuse is related to poverty does *not* mean that poor people in general abuse their children. Pelton argues persuasively that a classlessness notion of child abuse diverts our attention away from the real stresses of poverty and serves to maintain an ineffective psychiatric model of treatment. Addressing directly the relationship between social class and abuse allows consideration of important sociological variables and treatment strategies.

Numerous investigators have shown the inverse relationship between socioeconomic status and abuse rate (Gelles, 1980a; Giovannoni & Billingsley, 1970; S. Smith et al., 1975; Straus, 1979a). In other words, the lower the socioeconomic status, the higher the abuse rate. This relationship is found with a variety of indices of status, including income, education, and occupation.

Other, less obvious conditions associated with low socioeconomic status have been shown to be related to abuse. For example, cumulative life changes and stresses have been shown to be strongly related to child abuse (Conger et al., 1979; Gaines et al., 1978; Gelles, 1980a; Giovannoni & Billingsley, 1970; Justice & Duncan, 1976). Gelles also found that as the number of stressful life events increased, the likelihood of severe violence to children increased. Some events may be more stressful for poor families than middle class or wealthy families. As discussed earlier, Gelles' (1980a) national survey found that among the poorest families, each additional child increased the likelihood of abuse. Among middle income families, the risk of child abuse increased with each child up to seven, with no severe violence found in middle income families with eight or more children. There was no relationship between number of children and abuse rate for wealthy families.

Another important factor in the sociological model of child abuse is isolation from social supports and from community resources both inside and outside the family. As indicated in the previous chapter, isolation within the immediate family and from extended family, neighbors, and the broader community is a major factor in child abuse (Ayoub & Pfeifer, 1977; Egeland & Sroufe, 1981a, 1981b; Garbarino, 1977; Garbarino et al., 1977; Giovannoni & Billingsley, 1970; Hunter & Kilstrom, 1979; Hunter et al., 1978; Pfeifer & Ayoub, 1976; Straus, 1979a). Gelles (1982a) suggests that such isolation within both the family and larger community context reduces social controls that inhibit or negatively sanction family members for acts of violence. In the absence of such social controls, family violence can and does occur because there is no cost involved for engaging in violent acts.

A number of means for combating child abuse within a sociological model have been suggested including: change of our culture's acceptance of physical punishment as a child rearing technique, elimination of poverty, redistribution of social and economic power, reduction of job discrimination and unemployment, provision of better housing, provision of comprehensive family planning, family life education, and premarital counseling, and provision of neighborhood-based social services aimed at reducing environmental stresses on families and assisting them with relational problems (Albee, 1980; Almond, 1980; Gil, 1970; Kahn & Kamerman, 1980; Newberger & Bourne, 1978). While the factors these suggestions address are important causal agents in child abuse, they alone cannot account for the actual abusive behavior. The suggested interventions do appear critical for prevention, and are probably necessary components of an integrated attack involving both intervention and prevention strategies for the problem of child abuse.

It is unlikely that all possible stressors for a given family can ever be removed. Therefore, parents need to develop the skills for coping with these and other unpredictable stressors with which they may be confronted. Even if social supports and community resources are made available to families, family members need the knowledge and skills to make use of those supports and resources. The next model relates more directly to skill development interventions and thus to the change strategy described in this book.

SOCIAL SITUATIONAL MODEL

The social situational model represents a move towards a more preventive skill learning approach. It is derived from broadly based behavioral and social learning theory (Bandura, 1977). Taken together, the many versions of social situational theory as applied to child abuse focus upon all aspects of Keller and Erné's (1983) comprehensive approach to child abuse. It should be noted that any one social situational theory rarely addresses all the components.

This model focuses not only upon the characteristics of the participants in child abuse (i.e., the child victim and adult abuser) but also upon their interactional patterns, the interactional patterns of others in the environment, and the influence of the immediate and broader settings or social situations.

Until recently this model of child abuse was based more upon inferences derived from the general literature on aggression and parenting than upon direct controlled studies of abusive families. One of the advantages of research within the perspective of a social situational model is the emphasis upon direct assessment of problem behaviors through observation in relevant settings and the use of appropriate experimental designs for evaluating treatment effectiveness, even with single cases.

Research from the social situational perspective often examines the effects of punitive child rearing, inconsistent discipline, and punishment. Many studies, cited in the previous chapter, suggest a relationship between abusive behaviors of parents and the fact that they themselves were abused as children. This relationship is typically explained by the general literature on modeling of aggression (Bandura, 1973). The data demonstrate the effects of exposure to aggressive models on subsequent aggressive action. As discussed earlier, abuse rates are higher not only for those who themselves were victims of abuse but also for those who witnessed their own parents engaging in family violence (toward other children or each other).

Burgess and Conger provided a major contribution to the application of this model to the area of child abuse by identifying and measuring patterns of parent-child interaction that were strongly related to actual abusive behavior (Burgess, 1979; Burgess & Conger, 1978; Conger, 1982). As discussed before, their research and the research of others has shown that abusive parents have a lower overall rate of interaction with their children, lower rates of positive interactions, and higher rates of negative interactions (Burgess & Conger, 1978; Dietrich et al., 1980; Disbrow, Doerr, & Caulfield, 1977; Egeland & Brunnquell, 1979; Kimball et al., 1980; Reid et al., 1981). Abusive parents have also been observed to use ineffective and inconsistent punishment and methods of discipline, including high levels of physical punishment, demands, and threats (Kimball et al., 1980; Reid et al., 1981). Abused children also have higher rates of inappropriate and negative behaviors (Burgess, 1979; Burgess & Conger, 1978; Reid et al., 1981). Social isolation was also found to be related to parent-child interactions in a study by Wahler (1980). This study found that child-directed punitive behavior was consistently higher on days during which parental contact with friends was extremely low as compared to those days when friendship contacts were very high. Theoretically, social isolation can have other effects as well, such as a reduced likelihood of exposure to effective parenting models and a lack of feedback about parenting behavior.

Treatment approaches derived from the social situational model of child abuse make use of behavioral principles and techniques for changing inappropriate interactions within the family and for enhancing skills of family members. As indicated earlier, these approaches are characterized by direct measurement of problems and of change, with an emphasis upon evaluation of treatment effectiveness. Research on these treatment strategies, as with interventions derived from other models, has been primarily of the case study variety (without control groups), has not involved long-term followup of treatment effects, and has rarely examined transfer of treatment effects into the home situation.

There have been a number of reviews of behavioral interventions with abusive parents (Burgess, 1979; Cicchetti et al., 1978; Dubanoski, Evans, & Higuchi, 1978; Gambrill, 1983; Isaacs, 1982; Keller & Erné, 1983; Reid et al., 1981; Smith, 1984; Smith, Rachman, & Yule, 1984). Gambrill (1983) suggested that researchers using behavioral interventions too often use what she characterized as a "sharp shooter" approach (in which a single kind of intervention is used without consideration of the multiple factors involved in child abuse) or a "shotgun" approach (in which a broad package of procedures is used with little regard to the relevance of unique personal and situational deficits, resources, and stressors). Another criticism of behavioral interventions is that while there has been a rapid growth in cognitive behavioral theory and techniques, researchers using behavioral interventions have generally ignored the role of cognitions in abuse. In addition to providing instruction in child development in order to influence abusive parents' inappropriate cognitive expectations for their children's behaviors, such cognitions as empathic reactions of parents, parental attitudes and beliefs about their children, and self-efficacy (or a cognitive belief that one can change) could be addressed. Smith et al. (1984) present another criticism, arguing that behavioral researchers need to develop treatment strategies that can be easily adopted and used by workers in the child abuse field. Interventions using the social situational model often concentrate on building parenting skills, building anger control or self-control skills, building interpersonal skills, changing other parent behaviors, or changing the child's behavior. Research on each of these aspects will be presented in the following sections.

Building Parenting Skills

Parenting skills are the most frequent target of change strategies derived from the social situational model. One set of techniques involves the modification of parental disciplinary behavior to avoid the use of physically punitive tactics. Case studies have used many different strategies for reteaching parents to use nonassaultive control methods (Crozier & Katz, 1979; DeBortali-Tregerthan, 1979; Gilbert, 1976; Hughes, 1974; Jeffery, 1976; Jensen, 1976; Patterson, 1974; Polokow & Peabody, 1975; Reaveley & Gilbert, 1976; Sadler & Seyden, 1976; Sandler, Van Dercar, & Milhoan, 1978; Savino & Sanders, 1973; Stein & Gambrill, 1976; Tracy, Ballard, & Clark, 1975; Tracy & Clark, 1974; Wolfe & Sandler, 1981). Parents are given programmed texts on child management and then taught, through modeling or role playing, ways of increasing their children's prosocial (or socially desirable) behavior through positive reinforcement or decreasing their children's deviant behavior through alternatives to punishment. While these case reports typically indicate positive outcomes, they do not employ sufficient controls to allow a clear demonstration that the treatment was critical for bringing about changes in behavior. In addition, intervention often includes many procedures and many targets without full evaluation of specific treatment components or of specific effects on the various treatment targets. Crozier and Katz (1979), Sandler et al. (1978), and Stein and Gambrill (1976) did demonstrate long-term maintenance of behavior changes in this particular type of study.

Using a single case control design and a parent training approach assigning homework and giving direct instructions over an earplug to a mother being observed in a clinic setting, Wolfe et al. (1982) found a decrease in hostile verbal and physical parental behaviors both at home and in the clinic. In addition, there was an increase in praise and nurturing behavior. Effects were maintained over a 2-month followup. Burgess, Anderson, Shellenbach, and Conger (1981), also employing home-based training in positive child management techniques with a single case design, found similar appropriate gains in both parental and child behaviors. However, negative interactions did not change.

Control group designs have been used by a number of investigators using parent training in more appropriate disciplinary techniques. Stein, Gambrill, and Wiltse (1978) developed individually tailored written contracts between clients and social workers. The contracts involved specific behavioral training by staff and behavioral changes by parents. Of the problems dealt with, 44 percent involved parental disciplinary issues surrounding parent-child interactions. In 75 percent of the experimental group, identified problems were resolved, with the control group (receiving typical social services for abuse cases) having a 50 percent success rate. Christopherson et al. (1976) used home-based training involving modeling, rehearsal, and feedback (though with little specification of clients or of treatment content) and found that over 2 years only 18 percent of families had been referred again to protective services, as compared to 30 percent among families who refused the treatment program. On the average, treatment took 3 months per client. Reid et al. (1981), with a 4-week in-home parent training package, found a decrease in maternal and child aversive behaviors, but no change in fathers' behaviors. No followup was conducted. Wolfe, Sandler, and Kaufman (1981) used an intervention program consisting of parent training in child development (basic knowledge about developmental milestones) and in child management techniques, as well as problem solving skills and impulse control. A home visitor helped parents apply procedures they learned in a group training format. The total program was effective through a 10-week followup based upon home observations, caseworker reports, and parental self-reports. Child management skills increased, and fewer child problems were reported. Conger, Lahey, and Smith (1981) also used a comprehensive home intervention including instruction in child management, stress management, relaxation, couple relationships, and supportive relationships with the family. Using direct observation, they found fewer negative and more positive interactions, decreased maternal depression, and effective child compliance to parental requests. In another project involving 325 parents (abusive, neglectful, and at-risk) over a 2-year period, individually tailored programs were used (Lutzker, 1983; Lutzker, Frame, & Rice, 1982). In the 2 years, respectively 42 percent and 66 percent of the programs dealt with parent-child training. Success was reported in terms of case termination because all or "sufficient" goals were met and in terms of reoccurrence rates. Success appears better than for nonbehavioral programs, but evaluation was not specific to particular behavioral interventions. Smith and Rachman (1984) found successful changes in parental child management techniques for a number of families in their individually tailored behavioral programs, but they could not consider their program a success because of similar changes in their control group and a large number of experimental families who withdrew from the program out of noncooperation.

Building Anger Control or Self-control Skills

Since the social situational model suggests that many sources of stress and frustration present in the environment may serve as potential elicitors of anger and aggression, a second set of relevant intervention approaches is anger control and self-control techniques. These techniques include the reinforcement of incompatible nonangry responses, modeling and role playing of nonangry reactions, relaxation, systematic desensitization in the presence of the anger-evoking situations, and cognitive behavioral strategies including stress-inoculation, self-instruction, thought stopping, and self-control. (See Bandura, 1969, 1973, and Goldstein & Rosenbaum, 1982, for a thorough description and explanation of these methods.) The techniques have been shown to be effective with other aggressive populations, such as aggressive children (Gittelman, 1965) and antisocial adult males (Novaco, 1975; Rimm & Masters, 1979).

In a descriptive study of parents' experiences of anger towards their children, Frude and Goss (1979) explored the frequency of parents' feelings of anger towards their children, what the parents did to control those feelings of anger, and what situations seemed to provoke anger. Hitting children out of anger occurred frequently. Children's behavior that triggered anger included irritating actions, defiance, actions resulting in cost (such as breaking something valuable) or dangerous actions (such as setting a fire). Those parents who were able to stop themselves from losing control with their children described self-control methods like many of the techniques used in the professional literature. It seems possible that abusive parents may not possess or be able to consistently use these coping skills.

Case studies by Sandford and Tustin (1974) and Ambrose, Hazzard, and Haworth (1980) found only limited success with the application of these approaches to abusive parents. But a number of studies with controls successfully included one. or more of these strategies along with training in parenting skills (Conger et al., 1981; Denicola & Sandler, 1980; Lutzker, 1983; Lutzker et al., 1982; Smith & Rachman, 1984; Wolfe et al. 1981).

Denicola and Sandler (1980) employed a single case control design and examined the effects of self-control techniques on parent behaviors in the home. Using direct observation in the home, they found a reduction of total parental aversive behavior and an increase in parental prosocial behaviors (e.g., attention to child and approval). The abused children also showed an increase in prosocial and a decrease in aversive behavior. All effects were maintained at followup (1 to 3 months). Solomon (1977) used the Structured Learning approach described in this book to train abusive parents successfully in self-control skills (see Chapter Ten).

Building Interpersonal Skills

A third general approach within the social situational model addresses the isolation found among abusive parents. Specific targets might include general communication skills designed to reduce isolation both in the family and community. Such communication skills can help increase the abusive parent's use of family and community support systems. Various marital skills might represent another specific target of interpersonal skills training. Smith and Rachman (1984) found limited success with such training. Lutzker (1983) and Lutzker et al. (1982) recognized the importance of this target area, particularly the enhancement of marital skills, but chose to use marital counseling as the approach rather than behavioral interpersonal training. No indication of the success of marital counseling was presented.

Some investigators have suggested that group treatment might be more effective with abusive parents (as opposed to individual treatment) because of the social contact, friendships, and mutual support within the group. In addition to potential nonspecific benefits of group treatment (such as a universalization of the abuse phenomenon—"I'm not the only one who does this to children"), a group approach provides benefits specific to a social situational model. The group allows practice and feedback in the use of interpersonal skills, as well as many occasions for modeling the skills being taught. Numerous intervention programs have been conducted within group formats including the previously reported control group studies by Wolfe et al. (1981) and Solomon (1977).

Changing Other Parent Behaviors

In addition to the preceding targets for change and their associated change strategies, training within a social situational model has attempted to focus on other problems of abusing parents as well. For example, Reaveley and Gilbert (1979) focused on changing parents' attitudes towards their children and increasing their expression of positive feelings. They used modeling and a cognitive behavioral approach referred to as positive self-talk. While they did not analyze the effectiveness of specific treatment components in their case study report, they felt that such training was as important as training in specific parenting skills. Campbell, O'Brien, Bickett, and Lutzker (1983) used stress inoculation training for reducing mothers' tension headaches, arguing that these headaches might be part of the determinants of abuse. Unfortunately, they did not evaluate separate treatment components in a complex package including parent training, marital counseling, and financial planning. Control group studies by Stein et al. (1978) and Conger et al. (1981) demonstrated significant decreases in parental depression with the use of stress management training, along with other skills training approaches. Other researchers have argued that behavioral programs must address other areas of concern to abusive parents—including attitudes towards children, financial planning, job location, and alcoholism—in order to be successful (Gambrill, 1983; Smith, 1984; Smith et al., 1984).

Changing the Child's Behavior

Another set of techniques derived from the social situational model attempt to change the child's behavior. These approaches were developed largely by Patterson (1982) and his associates (Patterson & Cobb, 1971, 1973; Patterson & Reid, 1970), who taught parents nonpunitive ways for dealing with their children's behavior. They characterized parent-child interactions in aggressive families as part of a coercion process in which a child's aversive behavior serves to trigger parental punitive behavior that, in turn, results in a continuation and an increased intensity of the aversive interchange. This coercive process is the focus of the training procedures. Specific methods to change the child's behavior and prevent subsequent incidents of physical abuse include extinction, reinforcement of incompatible responses, timeout, verbal reasoning, communication skills, and negotiation skills. (See Bandura, 1969, 1973; Goldstein, 1983; and Jeffery, 1976, for fuller description of these techniques.) The case study by Stein and Gambrill (1976) and the control studies reported earlier (Burgess et al., 1981; Christopherson et al., 1976; Conger et al., 1981; Denicola & Sandler, 1980; Reid et al., 1981; Wolfe et al., 1981) all showed improvements in children's behavior and in interactional patterns, as well as in parental behavior.

No studies have attempted to address the prescriptive question of which approach or set of approaches from the social situational model (among the many available) works with which clients and problems under what set of conditions with which kind of therapist (Goldstein, 1978; Goldstein & Stein, 1976). The work that has been done suggests very strongly that these change strategies may be very effective with abusive parents and their families. Most research on these change strategies has demonstrated success in teaching parenting skills, in particular nonpunitive discipline techniques. In addition, research within the context of the skills training model has shown improvements in anger control and in interpersonal skills designed to reduce abusive parents' isolation. Training abusive parents in such skills has been shown to result in changes in children's behavior as well. There is also the strong suggestion in this literature that skills training is most effectively conducted in a group context. A strategy consistent with this model and designed to address these concerns in abusive families is presented in the remainder of this book.

Chapter Three

An Introduction to Structured Learning

As the previous chapters made clear, we view the physical abuse of a child as an event both best understood and best treated by careful attention to the abuser, the child, parent-child interactions, the family context, and the broader community and social context. Such a truly comprehensive approach to both cause and cure must focus, directly or indirectly, upon all of the actors who play a role in this damaging event. It is not enough, in our view, to simply attempt the difficult task of changing only the self-insight (psychiatric model), *or* social context (sociological model), *or* even the self-control (behavioral model) of the abusive parent. One must, we believe, seek to substantially impact on *all* relevant aspects of abusers' personal and interpersonal worlds—including self-control to be sure, but also their relationship with their children, spouses, neighbors, relatives, and important "others." We believe that intervention aimed at these several goals may result in parents who raise their children with nurturance, not abuse, who express anger appropriately, not destructively, and whose relationships with their spouses, relatives, and friends are satisfying and give a sense of interpersonal "in-touchness," rather than the more common—for abusive parents—sense of interpersonal isolation and impoverishment.

We have described a tall order here. It is, we believe, quite the proper prescription, but one not easily filled. We have sought to fill this order in our work, as will be detailed in subsequent chapters, by teaching a systematic curriculum of self-control, parenting, marital, and interpersonal skills to abusive parents. We have done so by means of a teaching method called Structured Learning, a method initiated by us in the early 1970s (Goldstein, 1973, 1981). At that time, most individually oriented intervention efforts directed towards assisting acting out, aggressive, or impulsive adults—often including abusive parents—grew from one of three treatment philosophies. These are the psychodynamic/psychoanalytic, the humanistic/nondirective, and behavior modification. Though each orientation differs from the others in several major respects, one shared assumption is that clients have within themselves, but have not expressed, the effective, satisfying, or healthy behaviors whose expression is among the goals of the treatment. It is assumed that skillful therapists in all three approaches can elicit these latent behaviors by reducing or removing obstacles to the behaviors. The psychoanalyst seeks to do this by calling forth and interpreting unconscious material blocking progress-relevant awareness. The humanistic, or nondirective, therapist seeks to free these behaviors by providing a warm, empathic, and accepting therapeutic environment. And the therapist using behavior modification attempts to see to it that when the latent desirable behaviors or approximations of them do occur, the client receives contingent reinforcement, thus increasing the probability that these behaviors will recur. Therefore, whether sought by means of therapeutic interpretation and working through, by provision of a benevolent therapeutic climate, or by offering contingent reward, all three approaches assume that somewhere within the individual's repertoire resides the desired, effective, sought-after goal behaviors.

PSYCHOLOGICAL SKILLS TRAINING

In the early 1970s an important new intervention approach began to emerge called psychological skills training. This approach is based upon different assumptions than the previous three. Instead of viewing clients as needing therapy, the psychological skills trainer assumed they lacked, were deficient in, or were at best weak in the skills necessary for effective interpersonal relationships and satisfying daily living.

The task of the skills trainer became, therefore, not interpretation, reflection, or reinforcement, but the active and deliberate teaching of desirable behaviors. Rather than an intervention between a patient and a psychotherapist, what emerged was training between a trainee and a psychological skills trainer.

Psychological skills training—a blending of both psychology and education—has its roots in the character education, moral education, and values clarification programs prominent in American education and in the century-long interest in the learning process at the heart of American psychology. It combines the teaching techniques of education and knowledge of the learning process from psychology to teach (not do therapy with) effective and satisfying personal and interpersonal behaviors to those deficient or weak in such skills.

Is it useful and appropriate to think of child abusing parents as skill deficient in this way? Considerable research evidence supports such a skill deficiency view, particularly with regard to those skills necessary for (1) *self-control* in anger-arousal situations, (2) competent, effective, and mutually satisfying *parenting* interactions, (3) *marital* satisfaction, and (4) generally effective *interpersonal* relationships with other people.

Research showing abusive parents to lack self-control skills includes observations and descriptions of them as deficient in self-control, impulse ridden, immature, and prone to chronically high levels of anger and overt aggression (Johnson & Morse, 1968; Keller & Erné, 1983; Zigler, 1980). These characteristics are based at least in part on the interaction of diverse social situational stresses, high levels of frustration, minimal social support to aid in reducing frustrations, and misinformation regarding the physical and emotional capacities of young children.

Research has also shown the broad array of attitudinal and behavioral proficiencies best described collectively as "parenting skills" to be another major area of deficiency for many abusive parents (Delissovoy, 1973; Garbarino, 1977; Johnson & Morse, 1968). For example, they are purported to rely too frequently and too energetically on corporal punishment and often literally do not know what to do instead. Although disciplining practices are usually singled out to illustrate parenting skills deficiency, the parent's inadequacy often extends to the full spectrum of physical, emotional, and interpersonal behaviors that constitute competent child rearing.

Marital relationships in the context of child abuse have been shown to be difficult, conflictual, and even abusive themselves (Giovannoni & Billingsley, 1970). Such marriages have been described as "disturbed" (Hellsten & Katila, 1965), "disastrous" (Gaylord, 1975), and "often violent" (Moore, 1975).

With their spouses, and with people in general, abusive parents also have been described as socially and interpersonally isolated (Alexander, 1972; Helfer & Kempe, 1976; Justice & Justice, 1976). Gottlieb (1980) comments:

> Without the requisite affiliative skills, social isolation is inevitable. . . . I am talking about such behaviors as listening, cooperating, considering the other person's perspective and needs, and conducting oneself in a manner that conveys respect and esteem for him or her. People who cut others off all the time, make constant demands for attention, and rarely reciprocate or disclose anything about themselves simply don't make good friends. (p. 50)

Abusive mothers, Zigler (1980) suggests, often are especially isolated and lacking in social support. More generally, it has been shown that abusive parents rarely have close ties with neighbors or relatives and very infrequently participate in community organizations (Giovannoni & Billingsley, 1970). Thus, in these four important skill-related realms of functioning—self-control, parenting ability, interpersonal relationships, marital relations—the abusive parent has been characteristically shown to be substantially deficient.

In planning and developing an intervention to assist any given type of client, such as abusive parents, it is ideally the case that "cure" follows "cause." That is, one's idea of what causes a given problem should strongly influence how one tries to intervene to reduce or eliminate it. If one believes, as some do, that child abuse grows from the disturbed inner life of the individual abusive parent, then one is likely to champion and prescribe an intervention targeted to the individual parent's psychodynamics as the best "cure." If the abuser is seen more as someone already possessing but not using the needed insights and behaviors necessary for adequate self-control, good parenting, and the like, one might ideally offer her a nondirective intervention, characterized by a warm, supportive, and nonprobing helper style. Or, instead, a behavior modification approach might fit best here, in which one waits for the appearance of, or shapes, already existing skill behaviors and then energetically seeks to reinforce them. But if, instead, one subscribes to the model put forth here—the behavior deficit model—the ideal prescription becomes a teaching intervention, that is, psychological skills training.

THE STRUCTURED LEARNING APPROACH TO PSYCHOLOGICAL SKILLS TRAINING

We seek in this book to describe our approach to psychological skills training in detail and justify our enthusiasm for offering it. We are in accord with Bandura's (1973) conclusion regarding the value of defining "cause" in behavior deficit terms, and "cure" as psychological skills training:

> The method that has yielded the most impressive results with diverse problems contains three major components. First, alternative modes of responses are repeatedly modeled, preferably by several people who demonstrate how the new style of behavior can be used in dealing with a variety of . . . situations. Second, learners are provided with necessary guidance and ample opportunities to practice the modeled behavior under favorable conditions until they perform it skillfully and spontaneously. The lat-

ter procedures are ideally suited for developing new social skills, but they are unlikely to be adopted unless they produce rewarding consequences. Arrangement of success experiences particularly for initial efforts at behaving differently, constitute the third component in this powerful composite method. . . . Given adequate demonstration, guided practice, and success experiences, this method is almost certain to produce favorable results. (p. 253)

Our approach to psychological skills training, Structured Learning, was strongly influenced by the same successful research outcomes underlying Bandura's conclusion (Bandura, 1969; Bryan & Test, 1967; Culbertson, 1957; King & Janis, 1956; Krumboltz & Schroeder, 1965). These investigations of both single educational and psychological techniques effective for remediating psychological skill deficiencies and combinations of such techniques led us to conclude that Structured Learning should optimally consist of (1) modeling, (2) role playing, (3) performance feedback, and (4) transfer training (Goldstein, 1973, 1981). In implementing these procedures, small groups of abusive parents, selected for their common skill deficits, are shown by videotape or live portrayals by the Structured Learning trainers a person (the model) performing the skill behaviors we wish the trainees to learn *(modeling)*. Each videotape or live modeling display consists of a series of vignettes portraying the concrete behavioral steps that constitute a given skill. In our work with abusive parents, the vignettes cover a broad spectrum of content areas relevant to the self-control, parenting, marital, and interpersonal demands of the trainees' real world. After the modeling display, trainees are given considerable opportunity and encouragement to rehearse or practice the behaviors that have been modeled, in a manner relevant to dealing with their own real-life problems *(role playing)*. They are provided with positive feedback, approval, or reward as their role playing behavior becomes more and more like the behavior of the model *(performance feedback)*. And they are exposed to these three processes in a way that ensures the likelihood that what they learn in the training setting will in fact be applied in a reliable manner at home or elsewhere *(transfer training)*. Homework assignments are made in which trainees are encouraged to practice their newly learned skills outside of the training setting in their real-life environments. These assignments are systematically reported upon in the subsequent session. The procedures used in Structured Learning will be discussed in more detail in Chapter Five.

This brief overview of Structured Learning, its roots and procedures, is designed to provide a flavor of its history and recent focus. In the chapters that follow, we will seek to provide the detail necessary to enable the reader to not only fully understand the substance of Structured Learning, but also to be able to actually conduct effective, skill-enhancing Structured Learning sessions with a wide variety of abusive parents.

Chapter Four

Preparing for Structured Learning

The purpose of this chapter is to provide the information needed to prepare effectively for conducting the Structured Learning group. The selection and preparation of both trainers and abusive parent trainees will be our major focus. We will also attend to such organizational decisions as the optimal number, length, timing, spacing, and location of the Structured Learning sessions themselves.

SELECTING TRAINERS

A wide variety of individuals have served successfully as Structured Learning trainers. Their formal educations have been especially varied, ranging from high school degree only through various graduate degrees. While formal training in a helping profession is both useful and relevant to becoming a competent Structured Learning trainer, we have found characteristics such as sensitivity, flexibility, and instructional talent to be considerably more important than formal education. We have made frequent and successful use of trainers best described as paraprofessionals, particularly with trainees from lower socioeconomic backgrounds. In Chapter Nine we describe in detail Alliance, the community organization at which most of our Structured Learning work with abusive parents during the past decade has been conducted. As part of that description, we comment on the role of Alliance's parent aides, who have served with great effectiveness as our paraprofessional Structured Learning trainers.

In general, we select trainers based upon the nature and demands of the Structured Learning group. Two types of trainer skills appear crucial for successfully conducting a Structured Learning group. The first might best be described as general trainer skills, that is, those skills requisite for success in almost any training or teaching effort. These include:

1. Oral communication and teaching ability,
2. Flexibility and capacity for resourcefulness,
3. Enthusiasm,

4. Ability to work under pressure,
5. Interpersonal sensitivity,
6. Listening skills,
7. Knowledge of their subject (good parenting behaviors, sources of marital satisfaction, etc.).

The second type of necessary skills is specific trainer skills, that is, those skills relevant to Structured Learning in particular. These include:

1. Knowledge of Structured Learning—its background, procedures, and goals;
2. Ability to orient both trainees and supporting staff to Structured Learning;
3. Ability to plan and present live modeling displays;
4. Ability to initiate and sustain role playing;
5. Ability to present material in concrete, behavioral form;
6. Ability to deal with group management problems effectively;
7. Accuracy and sensitivity in providing corrective feedback.

How can we tell if potential trainers are skilled enough to become effective group leaders? We use behavioral observation, seeing how competently potential trainers lead mock and then actual Structured Learning groups during the preparation phase.

PREPARING TRAINERS

As this entire book makes clear, we strongly believe in learning by doing. Our chief means of preparing trainers for Structured Learning group leadership is, first, to have them participate in an intensive 2-day workshop designed to provide the knowledge and experiences needed for a beginning competence at being a trainer. In the workshop, we use Structured Learning to teach Structured Learning. First, we assign reading materials, such as this book, for background information. Next, trainees observe skilled and experienced Structured Learning group leaders model the central modeling display presentation, role playing, performance feedback, and transfer training procedures, which constitute the core elements of the Structured Learning session. Then, workshop participants role play in pairs these group leadership behaviors and receive detailed feedback from the workshop leaders and others in the training group regarding the degree to which their group leadership behaviors matched or departed from those modeled by the workshop leaders. To try to ensure that workshop learning transfers smoothly and fully to agency functioning, regular and continuing supervisory sessions are held after the workshop with the newly created Structured Learning group leaders. These booster, monitoring, and supervision meetings, when added to the several opportunities available for trainer performance evaluation during the workshop itself, provide a very large sample of behaviors upon which to base a fair and appropriate trainer selection decision.

SELECTING TRAINEES

Who belongs in the Structured Learning group? We have long held that no therapy or training approach is optimal for all clients, and that our effectiveness as helpers or trainers will grow to the degree that we become prescriptive in our helping efforts (Goldstein, 1978; Goldstein & Stein, 1976). As noted earlier, Structured Learning grew originally from a behavior deficit view of asocial and antisocial behavior, including child abuse. If abusive behavior, at least in large part, is due to lack of parental ability in self-control, parenting, marital, and general interpersonal skills, then our selection goal is defined for us. The Structured Learning group should consist of persons who have abused their child or children and who are, or believe themselves to be, weak or deficient in one or more of the four key skill areas noted. Largely or entirely irrelevant to this selection decision are most of the usual bases for treatment or training selection decisions. If the clients abuse their children, are skill deficient, and possess a few very basic group participation skills, we are largely unconcerned with their age, sex, race, occupation, social class or, within very broad limits, even their mental health. At times we have had to exclude persons who were severely emotionally disturbed, too hyperactive for a 30-minute session, or so developmentally disabled that they lacked the rudimentary memory and imagery abilities necessary for adequate group participation. But such persons have been relatively few and quite far between. Thus, while Structured Learning is not a prescription designed for all abusive parents, its range of appropriate use is nevertheless quite broad.

ASSESSING TRAINEES' SKILLS

If skill deficit is the main basis for deciding whether an individual should be offered Structured Learning, how will the person's level of skill deficit be determined? We have found it useful to estimate levels of skill deficiency by employing, alone or in combination, four methods of assessment: interviews, direct observation, behavioral testing, and skill checklists.

Interviews

In each skill area—self-control, parenting, marital, and interpersonal—the abusive parent has an impact upon other people—for better or, more usually, for worse. Other people are prime sources for information about the parent's skill proficiency or deficiency. Thus, in addition to the obvious value of asking the parent, useful information may be obtained, with the parent's permission, from interviews conducted with the abuser's spouse, neighbors, relatives, friends, and, if possible and appropriate, the abused children involved.

Direct Observation

There very often exists, intentionally or otherwise, important discrepancies between what people say they do, or would do, in a given situation and how they actually behave. Valuable information about skill proficiency or deficiency may be obtained by actually observing the child abusing parent function in her own home or elsewhere in her interpersonal world. What does she actually *do* when her children cry, yell, spit up, soil their diapers, hit friends, turn up the TV, awaken late at night, and so forth? We have been fortunate in this regard at Alliance because a primary responsibility of the parent aide staff (the same people who serve as our Structured Learning trainers) is to spend a considerable number of hours each week in the parent's home, assisting the parent in a variety of ways. This has contributed greatly to an accurate assessment of parent skill levels.

Behavioral Testing

One weakness of direct observation as a method of obtaining skill deficit information is that circumstances that allow the parent to show whether or not she possesses a given skill and is willing and able to use it may not occur during the period of observation. While the tester or observer is present, baby may not cry, problems may not reach a climax, husband may not start an argument with wife. When direct observation of skill use is impossible, an alternative is behavioral testing. This assessment approach involves creating, by role play, simulation, play acting, or in imagination, the types of situations that in real life would require competent skill use for solution, and then observing what the parent does. While the artificial nature of behavioral testing compared to direct observation in the home is a drawback, it can be applied to all potential trainees in a standardized manner. Well chosen and realistically portrayed situations can elicit important information about skill proficiency and deficiency.

Skill Checklists

We have urged that real-world others be interviewed and that the parent's skill-relevant behavior be observed in natural and contrived environments. But what of information from the parent herself?

We have consistently found skill deficiency information obtained directly from the abusive parent to be a particularly worthwhile part of the assessment picture. It tells us not only in which skills the parent estimates she is strong or weak, but via the act of sharing this information with us, also lets us know a bit about her motivation to change. Information obtained from the parent can also be compared to information from other sources to determine suitability for training. For example, the parent whom everyone else sees as highly skill deficient, but who sees herself as a near-perfect example of self-control, parenting, marital, and interpersonal skills would be an especially poor choice for inclusion in a Structured Learning group. To obtain self-report information from abusive parents in the four core skill areas, we have developed the Structured Learning Skill Checklist for Trainees, which appears on pages 53–55. This checklist, and all other forms in this book, may be copied for use with abusive parents.

Parallel checklist information about an individual may be obtained from others, such as the Structured Learning trainer, close relatives or friends, or other people having regular opportunities to observe the trainee in real-world interactions. The Structured Learning Skill Checklist for Trainers is provided for this purpose. It corresponds exactly in its list of skills to the trainee's form and appears on pages 56–58.

Checklist results have proven useful for three different aspects of the preparation phase of Structured Learning. These are trainee selection, trainee grouping, and negotiating the skill curriculum.

Checklist results and trainee selection. In deciding whether or not to place a given abusive parent in a Structured Learning group, it will be helpful to have an overall picture of her level of deficiency across all 24 of the skills that constitute the Structured Learning core curriculum for abusive parents. The Skill Checklist Summary (page 59) provides this opportunity. It may be used to summarize the parent's self-reports or the reports of the trainer or others on the skill checklists. The checklist summary permits recording not only of the trainee's skill levels before Structured Learning (from the pretest skill checklist, to be recorded in column 1) but also her skill levels following Structured Learning (from the posttest skill checklist, to be recorded in column 2). The difference between these scores (to be recorded in column 3) provides a rough index of either self-reported or other-reported change in the trainee's skill levels.

Checklist results and trainee grouping.   We noted earlier that the trainees assigned to any given Structured Learning group will ideally possess shared skill deficiencies. While their skill deficiencies will rarely, if ever, be identical, common weaknesses are essential to the meaningful progress of the group. Except on unusual and infrequent occasions, we do not want a trainee involved in observing a modeling display, role playing, and receiving feedback on a skill he is competent in already. To facilitate the grouping process, the trainer uses the Skill Training Grouping Chart (page 60). The trainees' names may be entered in the spaces at the top of each column and their skill levels—as reported on the checklist itself or the checklist summary—may be entered next to each skill within the columns. In this manner, the chart provides a visual summary of skill proficiency and deficiency for all skills across all trainees. The trainer may then readily group parents according to shared skill deficits by scanning the chart for low ratings (1s or 2s) within the same skill group and assigning trainees to groups according to similar score patterns.

Checklist results and negotiating the curriculum.   As is true for all teaching and learning efforts, whether or not a student learns what is being taught is partly a result of his capacity to learn and partly a result of his motivation. No matter how refined and polished the procedures that make up Structured Learning and no matter how high the intelligence level of its trainees, skill learning will not occur unless the trainees are motivated to learn.

Many things will help motivate the trainee in the Structured Learning sessions: encouraging, pleasant, and competent trainers; comfortable surroundings for the sessions; friendships formed within the training group; provision of transportation to the training agency and babysitters for youngsters left at home; and so forth. But the crucial influence on motivation, far surpassing all other influences combined, is whether the trainee believes the skill to be taught will be valuable in his life. If he doesn't believe this, the skills training effort will crawl forward. It is vital that the skills chosen for instruction, in the early meetings in particular, emphasize those that trainees consciously want, strongly desire, and admit to serious deficiency in.

To reach this curriculum sequencing goal without at the same time denying the substantial expertise of the trainer regarding which skills should be taught in which order, the curriculum needs to be negotiated. Using the completed skill checklist or checklists or

checklist summary, the trainer and trainee present, discuss, negoti-
ate, and come to agreement upon which skills in what order would
be the best learning sequence for that trainee. This negotiation process avoids the dual danger of turning curriculum setting into either
a cafeteria for the trainee, in which he picks whichever skills he wants
with no input from the trainer, or a dictatorship by the trainer, in
which the trainer sets the curriculum with no trainee input. Both par-
ties must be heard to assure both wise selection and high levels of
trainee motivation. Negotiating the curriculum in this manner can
begin on a presession basis with individual parents and be continued
periodically with the group as a whole.

GROUP ORGANIZATION

The preparation phase of the Structured Learning group is completed
by attention to those organizational details necessary for a smoothly
initiated, appropriately paced, and highly instructional group to
begin. Factors to be considered in organizing the group are: number
of trainees, number of trainers, number of sessions, spacing of sessions, and length and location of sessions.

Number of Trainees

Since trainee behavior in a Structured Learning group may vary
greatly from person to person and group to group, it is not appropriate that we recommend a single, specific number of trainees as optimal. Ideally, the number of trainees will permit all to role play, will
lead to optimal levels of group interaction, and will provide a diverse
source of performance feedback opportunities. In our experience
with abusive parents, these goals have most usually been met when
the group's size was six to nine trainees.

Number of Trainers

The role playing and feedback that make up most of each Structured
Learning session are a series of "action-reaction" sequences in which
effective skill behaviors are first rehearsed (role played) and then cri-
tiqued (feedback). Thus, the trainer must both lead and observe. We
have found that one trainer is hard pressed to do both of these tasks
well at the same time, and we strongly recommend that each session
be led by a team of two trainers. One trainer can usually pay special
attention to the main actor, helping the actor "set the stage" and enact

the skill's behavioral steps. While this is occurring, the other trainer can attend to the remainder of the group and help them as they observe and evaluate the unfolding role play. The two trainers can then exchange these responsibilities on the next role play.

Number of Sessions

Structured Learning groups typically seek to cover one skill in one or two sessions. The central task is to make certain that every trainee in the group role plays the given skill correctly at least once, preferably more than once. Most Structured Learning groups have met this curriculum plan by holding sessions once or twice per week. Groups have varied greatly in the total number of meetings they have held. Some have targeted only a single skill group (six skills), and thus met on a short-term, time-limited basis just to complete such a shortened curriculum. Other groups have held enough meetings to cover the 24 skills of the core curriculum and then continued on even further to additional skills from the supplementary curriculum listed later in this book (Chapter Six) or from the original adult (Goldstein, Sprafkin, & Gershaw, 1976) or adolescent (Goldstein, Sprafkin, Gershaw, & Klein, 1980) curricula.

Spacing of Sessions

The goal of Structured Learning is not merely skill learning or acquisition; much more important is skill transfer. Performance of the skill in the training setting is desired, but performance of it at home is crucial. Several aspects of Structured Learning, discussed especially in the chapter that follows, are designed to enhance the likelihood of such skill transfer. Session spacing is one such factor. As will be described later, after the trainee role plays successfully in the group and receives thorough performance feedback, he is assigned homework, that is, the task of carrying out in the real world the skill he just performed correctly in the group. In order to ensure ample time and opportunity to carry out this very important task, Structured Learning sessions must be scheduled at least a few days apart.

Length and Location of Sessions

One-hour sessions are the typical Structured Learning format, though both somewhat briefer and somewhat longer sessions have been successful. In general, the session goal that must be met is successful role playing and clarifying feedback for all participants, be it in 45 minutes, an hour, or an hour and a half.

In most agencies, a reasonably quiet and reasonably comfortable office, classroom, or similar setting can be found or created in which the Structured Learning groups may be conducted. We suggest no special requirements for the meeting place beyond those that make sense for any kind of group instruction—that it be free of distraction; at least minimally equipped with chairs, chalkboard, adequate lighting; and, if possible, that there be a coffee pot simmering on a stove or hot plate. How shall the room be arranged? Again, no single, fixed pattern is required, but one functional and comfortable layout is the horseshoe or U-shaped arrangement, which we have often employed—sometimes with and sometimes without tables. Figure 1 depicts this room arrangement. Note how in this group arrangement all observing trainees and the main actor can watch the trainer point to the given skill's behavioral steps written on the chalkboard while the role play is taking place. In this manner, any necessary prompting is provided immediately and at the same time as the role play serves as an additional modeling display for observing trainees.

Figure 1. A Functional Room Arrangement for Structured Learning

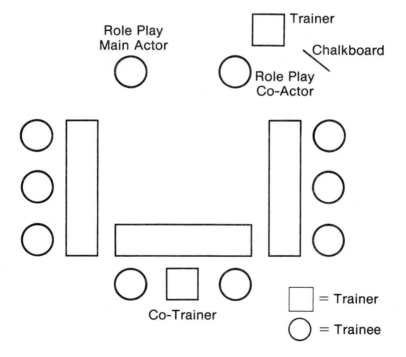

MEETING WITH THE TRAINEES BEFORE THE FIRST SESSION

A final step that must be taken before holding the first session of a new Structured Learning group is preparing the trainees who have been selected for what they ought to expect and what will be expected of them. What this premeeting might include follows.

1. *Describing what the purposes of the group will be as they relate to the trainee's specific skill deficits.* For example, the trainer might say, "Remember when Billy woke up crying at 2:00 a.m. last week, and you got so upset and angry that you wound up squeezing him hard and causing him to cry even more? Well, in Structured Learning, you'll be able to learn how to control those feelings and handle Billy and yourself in a way that calms down the situation."

2. *Describing briefly the procedure that will be used.* While we believe that trainees typically will not have a full understanding of what Structured Learning is and what it can accomplish until after the group has begun and they have experienced it, verbal, pregroup structuring of procedures is a useful beginning. It conveys at least a part of the information necessary to help trainees know what to expect. The trainer might say, "In order to learn to handle these problem situations better, we're going to see and hear some examples of how different parents handle them well. Then you will actually take turns trying some of these ways right here. We'll let you know how you did, and you'll have a chance to practice on your own."

3. *Describing some of the hoped-for benefits of active trainee participation in the group.* If the trainer has information from a trainee—for example, a completed Structured Learning Skill Checklist—the possible benefits described might appropriately be improved proficiency in the particular Structured Learning skills in which the trainee rates herself as especially deficient.

4. *Describing group rules.* These rules include whatever the trainer believes the group members must adhere to in order to function smoothly and effectively with regard to attendance, punctuality, confidentiality, completion of homework assignments, and so forth. At this premeeting stage, rule structuring should be brief and tentative. Reserve a fuller discussion of this matter for the group's first session, in which all members can be encouraged to participate, and in which rule changes can be made by consensus if such changes are the will of the group.

Structured Learning Skill Checklist for Trainees

Name: _____ Date: _____

There are several skills people need to use almost every day in order to get along with other people and feel good about themselves. We would like to know which skills you feel you are good at and which skills you feel you are not good at.

Below you will find a list of skills. Read each skill carefully and then put a circle around the number that describes best how good you are at using the skill.

> Circle 1, if you are *never* good at it.
> Circle 2, if you are *seldom* good at it.
> Circle 3, if you are *sometimes* good at it.
> Circle 4, if you are *often* good at it.
> Circle 5, if you are *always* good at it.

Try to rate yourself for every skill. If you do not understand a word or are unsure about what a skill description means, please ask the person who gave you this survey. There are no right or wrong answers, we are only interested in finding out your feelings about your skills. Please do not skip any items. Thank you for your cooperation.

	Never	Seldom	Sometimes	Often	Always
Group I					
1. **Identifying and Labeling Your Emotions:** Trying to recognize what emotions you are feeling.	1	2	3	4	5
2. **Relaxing:** Trying to calm yourself down and feel less tense.	1	2	3	4	5
3. **Using Self-control:** Controlling your temper before things get out of hand.	1	2	3	4	5
4. **Concentrating on a Task:** Making those preparations that will help you get something done efficiently.	1	2	3	4	5
5. **Deciding What Caused a Problem:** Finding out whether you or someone else has caused an event to happen.	1	2	3	4	5

	Never	Seldom	Sometimes	Often	Always
6. **Setting Problem Priorities:** Deciding which problem is most pressing so that you can work on it and not spend your time on less important matters.	1	2	3	4	5

Group II

7. **Expressing Anger:** Letting someone know you feel angry in a direct and honest manner.	1	2	3	4	5
8. **Expressing Affection:** Letting someone know that you care about him.	1	2	3	4	5
9. **Evaluating Your Abilities:** Looking carefully and honestly at your abilities in order to realistically decide just how strong or weak you are in those abilities.	1	2	3	4	5
10. **Making a Decision:** Deciding on realistic plans that you feel will be in your best interest.	1	2	3	4	5
11. **Setting a Goal:** Deciding what you want to accomplish, how to do it, and whether it is realistic.	1	2	3	4	5
12. **Helping Others:** Making a situation easier for others when they are having difficulty handling a situation themselves.	1	2	3	4	5

Group III

13. **Responding to the Feelings of Others:** Trying to figure out what the other person is feeling and then telling him what your impressions are.	1	2	3	4	5
14. **Responding to a Complaint:** Trying to arrive at a fair solution to someone's justified complaint.	1	2	3	4	5
15. **Responding to Anger:** Trying to understand the other person's anger and letting him know that you are trying.	1	2	3	4	5

		Never	Seldom	Sometimes	Often	Always

16. **Responding to Contradictory Messages:** Recognizing and taking steps to clear up the confusion that results when someone tells you one thing but, at the same time, says or does things that indicate that he means something else.   1 2 3 4 5

17. **Preparing for a Stressful Conversation:** Planning what you think will be the most effective presentation of your point of view.   1 2 3 4 5

18. **Negotiating:** Arriving at a plan that satisfies both yourself and another person who has taken a different position.   1 2 3 4 5

Group IV

19. **Starting a Conversation:** Talking to someone about light topics and then leading into more serious topics.   1 2 3 4 5

20. **Expressing Appreciation:** Letting another person know that you are grateful for something that he has done for you.   1 2 3 4 5

21. **Asking for Help:** Requesting that someone who is qualified help you in handling a difficult situation that you have not been able to manage yourself.   1 2 3 4 5

22. **Giving Instructions:** Clearly explaining to someone how you would like a specific task done.   1 2 3 4 5

23. **Being Assertive:** Standing up for yourself by letting people know what you want, how you feel, or what you think about something.   1 2 3 4 5

24. **Responding to Failure:** Figuring out what went wrong and what you can do about it so that you can be more successful in the future.   1 2 3 4 5

Structured Learning Skill Checklist for Trainers

Trainee's Name: _____   Date: _____

Rater's Name: _____

The purpose of this checklist is to gather information about the skill strengths and weaknesses of the person you are rating as you see them. This information will be useful in assigning trainees to Structured Learning groups, and in deciding which skills to teach.

Please rate the person whose name appears at the top of this page by reading each skill carefully and circling the number that, in your estimate, best describes how good the person is at using the skill.

Circle 1, if the person is *never* good at using the skill.
Circle 2, if the person is *seldom* good at using the skill.
Circle 3, if the person is *sometimes* good at using the skill.
Circle 4, if the person is *often* good at using the skill.
Circle 5, if the person is *always* good at using the skill.

Please do not skip any items. Thank you for your cooperation.

	Never	Seldom	Sometimes	Often	Always
Group I. Self-control Skills					
1. **Identifying and Labeling Your Emotions:** Trying to recognize what emotions you are feeling.	1	2	3	4	5
2. **Relaxing:** Trying to calm yourself down and feel less tense.	1	2	3	4	5
3. **Using Self-control:** Controlling your temper before things get out of hand.	1	2	3	4	5
4. **Concentrating on a Task:** Making those preparations that will help you get something done efficiently.	1	2	3	4	5
5. **Deciding What Caused a Problem:** Finding out whether you or someone else has caused an event to happen.	1	2	3	4	5

	Never	Seldom	Sometimes	Often	Always
6. **Setting Problem Priorities:** Deciding which problem is most pressing so that you can work on it and not spend your time on less important matters.	1	2	3	4	5

Group II. Parenting Skills

	Never	Seldom	Sometimes	Often	Always
7. **Expressing Anger:** Letting someone know you feel angry in a direct and honest manner.	1	2	3	4	5
8. **Expressing Affection:** Letting someone know that you care about him.	1	2	3	4	5
9. **Evaluating Your Abilities:** Looking carefully and honestly at your abilities in order to realistically decide just how strong or weak you are in those abilities.	1	2	3	4	5
10. **Making a Decision:** Deciding on realistic plans that you feel will be in your best interest.	1	2	3	4	5
11. **Setting a Goal:** Deciding what you want to accomplish, how to do it, and whether it is realistic.	1	2	3	4	5
12. **Helping Others:** Making a situation easier for others when they are having difficulty handling a situation themselves.	1	2	3	4	5

Group III Marital Skills

	Never	Seldom	Sometimes	Often	Always
13. **Responding to the Feelings of Others:** Trying to figure out what the other person is feeling and then telling him what your impressions are.	1	2	3	4	5
14. **Responding to a Complaint:** Trying to arrive at a fair solution to someone's justified complaint.	1	2	3	4	5
15. **Responding to Anger:** Trying to understand the other person's anger and letting him know that you are trying.	1	2	3	4	5

	Never	Seldom	Sometimes	Often	Always
16. **Responding to Contradictory Messages:** Recognizing and taking steps to clear up the confusion that results when someone tells you one thing, but at the same time, says or does things that indicate that he means something else.	1	2	3	4	5
17. **Preparing for a Stressful Conversation:** Planning what you think will be the most effective presentation of your point of view.	1	2	3	4	5
18. **Negotiating:** Arriving at a plan that satisfies both yourself and another person who has taken a different position.	1	2	3	4	5

Group IV. Interpersonal Skills

	Never	Seldom	Sometimes	Often	Always
19. **Starting a Conversation:** Talking to someone about light topics and then leading into more serious topics.	1	2	3	4	5
20. **Expressing Appreciation:** Letting another person know that you are grateful for something that he has done for you.	1	2	3	4	5
21. **Asking for Help:** Requesting that someone who is qualified help you in handling a difficult situation that you have not been able to manage yourself.	1	2	3	4	5
22. **Giving Instructions:** Clearly explaining to someone how you would like a specific task done.	1	2	3	4	5
23. **Being Assertive:** Standing up for yourself by letting people know what you want, how you feel, or what you think about something.	1	2	3	4	5
24. **Responding to Failure:** Figuring out what went wrong and what you can do about it so that you can be more successful in the future.	1	2	3	4	5

Skill Checklist Summary

Instructions: Write in the ratings (from the skill checklist) as well as the date on which the pre- or posttesting was accomplished. After posttesting is completed, record the difference between the pre- and posttest scores in the last column with the appropriate + or − to indicate change in performance on each skill. Since the skills are *not* equivalent in difficulty, do *not* add or average change scores for the skills involved.

Trainee's Name: _____

	Pretest Score / Date	Posttest Score / Date	Performance Change Posttest-Pretest
Group I. Self-control Skills			
1. Identifying and Labeling Your Emotions			
2. Relaxing			
3. Using Self-control			
4. Concentrating on a Task			
5. Deciding What Caused a Problem			
6. Setting Problem Priorities			
Group II. Parenting Skills			
7. Expressing Anger			
8. Expressing Affection			
9. Evaluating Your Abilities			
10. Making a Decision			
11. Setting a Goal			
12. Helping Others			
Group III. Marital Skills			
13. Responding to the Feelings of Others			
14. Responding to a Complaint			
15. Responding to Anger			
16. Responding to Contradictory Messages			
17. Preparing for a Stressful Conversation			
18. Negotiating			
Group IV. Interpersonal Skills			
19. Starting a Conversation			
20. Expressing Appreciation			
21. Asking for Help			
22. Giving Instructions			
23. Being Assertive			
24. Responding to Failure			

Skill Training Grouping Chart

Instructions: Write in the ratings (from the skill checklist or checklist summary) and the date the skill was covered. Ratings 1 and 2 generally indicate a skill deficit. For grouping purposes, trainees having low ratings on a number of skills within a skill group should be placed together in the same group.

	Trainee's Name				
Group I. Self-control Skills					
1. Identifying and Labeling Your Emotions					
2. Relaxing					
3. Using Self-control					
4. Concentrating on a Task					
5. Deciding What Caused a Problem					
6. Setting Problem Priorities					
Group II. Parenting Skills					
7. Expressing Anger					
8. Expressing Affection					
9. Evaluating Your Abilities					
10. Making a Decision					
11. Setting a Goal					
12. Helping Others					
Group III. Marital Skills					
13. Responding to the Feelings of Others					
14. Responding to a Complaint					
15. Responding to Anger					
16. Responding to Contradictory Messages					
17. Preparing for a Stressful Conversation					
18. Negotiating					
Group IV. Interpersonal Skills					
19. Starting a Conversation					
20. Expressing Appreciation					
21. Asking for Help					
22. Giving Instructions					
23. Being Assertive					
24. Responding to Failure					

Chapter Five

Conducting the Structured Learning Group

The purpose of this chapter is to provide a detailed, step-by-step description of the procedures that constitute the Structured Learning session. The opening session will be considered first. The elements of this session that get the Structured Learning group off to a good start will be emphasized. The chapter then turns to the procedures that constitute the bulk of most Structured Learning sessions—modeling, role playing, performance feedback, and transfer training. Then an outline that can be followed for sessions after the first is presented.

THE OPENING SESSION

The opening session is designed to create a safe, nurturing, non-threatening environment for trainees, stimulate their interest in the group, and give more detailed information to them than was provided in their individual orientations. The trainers open the session with a brief familiarization period of warmup, to help participants become comfortable when interacting with the group leaders and with one another. Content for this initial phase should be interesting and non-threatening to the trainees. Next, trainers introduce the Structured Learning program by providing trainees with a brief description of what skill training is about. Typically this introduction covers such topics as the importance of interpersonal skills for effective and satisfying living, examples of skills that will be taught, and how these skills can be useful to trainees in their everyday lives. It is often helpful to expand this discussion of everyday skill use to emphasize the importance of the undertaking and the personal relevance of learning the skill to the participants. The specific training procedures (modeling, role playing, performance feedback, and transfer training) are then described at a level that the group can easily understand. We recommend that trainers describe procedures briefly, with the expectation that trainees will understand them more fully once they have actually participated in their use. A detailed outline of the procedures that ideally make up this opening session follows.

Outline of Opening Session Procedures

A. Introductions
    1. Trainers introduce themselves.
    2. Trainers invite trainees to introduce themselves. As a way of relaxing trainees and beginning to familiarize them with one another, the trainer can elicit from each trainee some non-private information such as neighborhood of residence, occupation, special interests or hobbies, and so forth.
B. Overview of Structured Learning
    Although some or all of this material may have been discussed in earlier, individual meetings with trainees, a portion of the opening session should be devoted to a presentation and group discussion of the purposes, procedures, and potential benefits of Structured Learning. The discussion of the group's purposes should stress the probable remediation of those skill deficits that trainees in the group are aware of, concerned about, and eager to change. The procedures that make up the typical Structured Learning session should be explained again and discussed with give and take from the group. The language used to explain the procedures should be geared to the trainees' level of understanding, that is, "show," "try," "discuss," and "practice" respectively for "modeling," "role playing," "performance feedback," and "transfer training." Perhaps heaviest stress at this point should be placed on presenting and examining the potential benefits to trainees of their participation in Structured Learning. Concrete examples of the diverse ways that skill proficiencies could, and probably will, have a positive effect on the lives of trainees should be the focus of this effort.
C. Group Rules
    The rules that will govern participation in the Structured Learning group should be presented by the trainers during the opening session. If appropriate, this presentation should permit and encourage group discussion designed to give members a sense of participation in the group's decision making. That is, members should be encouraged to accept and live by those rules they agree with and seek to alter those they wish to change. Group rules may be necessary and appropriate concerning attendance, lateness, size of the group, and time and place of the meetings. This is also a good time to provide reassurance to group members about concerns they may have such as confidentiality, embarrassment, and fear of performing.

Following introductions, the overview of Structured Learning, and the presentation of group rules, the trainers should proceed to introducing and modeling the group's first skill, conducting role plays on that skill, giving performance feedback, and encouraging transfer training. These activities make up all of the subsequent Structured Learning sessions.

MODELING

The modeling displays presented to trainees should depict the behavioral steps that constitute the skill being taught in a clear and unambiguous manner. All of the steps making up the skill should be modeled, in the correct sequence. Generally, the modeling will consist of live vignettes enacted by the two trainers, although trainees may be involved in the modeling displays in some instances. (If available, audio or audiovisual modeling displays, instead of live modeling, may be presented.) When two trainers are not available, a reasonably skillful trainee may serve as a model along with the trainer. In all instances, it is especially important to rehearse the vignettes carefully prior to the group meeting, making sure that all of the skill's steps are enacted correctly and in the proper sequence.

Trainers should plan their modeling displays carefully. Content should be selected that is relevant to the immediate life situations of the trainees in the group. At least two examples should be modeled for each skill so that trainees are exposed to skill use in different situations. Thus, two or more different content areas are depicted. We have found that trainers usually do not have to write out scripts for the modeling displays but can instead plan their roles and likely responses in outline form and rehearse them in their preclass preparations. These modeling display outlines should incorporate the guidelines that follow:

1. Use at least two examples of different situations for each demonstration of a skill. If a given skill is taught in more than one group meeting, develop two more new modeling displays.
2. Select situations that are relevant to the trainees' real-life circumstances.
3. The main actor, that is, the person enacting the behavioral steps of the skill, should be portrayed as a person reasonably similar in age, socioeconomic background, verbal ability, and other salient characteristics to the people in the Structured Learning group.
4. Modeling displays should depict only one skill at a time. All extraneous content should be eliminated.

5. All modeling displays should depict all the behavioral steps of the skill being modeled in the correct sequence.
6. All displays should depict positive outcomes. Displays should always end with reinforcement to the model.

In order to help trainees attend to the skill enactments, Skill Cards, which contain the name of the skill being taught and its behavioral steps, are distributed prior to the modeling displays. Trainees are told to watch and listen closely as the models portray the skill. Particular care should be given to helping trainees identify the behavioral steps as they are presented in the context of the modeling vignettes. Trainers should also remind the trainees that in order to depict some of the behavioral steps in certain skills, the actors will occasionally be "thinking out loud" statements that would ordinarily be thought silently, and that this process is done to facilitate learning.

ROLE PLAYING

Following the modeling display, discussion should focus on relating the modeled skill to the lives of trainees. Trainers should invite comments on the behavioral steps and how these steps might be useful in real-life situations that trainees encounter. It is most helpful to focus on current and future skill use rather than only on past events or general issues involving the skill. Role playing in Structured Learning is intended to serve as behavioral rehearsal or practice for future use of the skill. Role playing of past events that have little relevance for future situations is of limited value to trainees. However, discussion of past events involving skill use can be relevant in stimulating trainees to think of times when a similar situation might occur in the future. The hypothetical future situation rather than a reenactment of the past event would be selected for role playing.

Once a trainee has described a situation in her own life in which the skill might be helpful, that trainee is designated the main actor. She chooses a second trainee (the co-actor) to play the role of the other person (mother, peer, child, etc.) in her life who is relevant to the situation. The trainee should be urged to pick as a co-actor someone who resembles the real-life person in as many ways as possible—physically, expressively, etc. The trainers then elicit from the main actor any additional information needed to set the stage for role playing. To make role playing as realistic as possible, the trainers should obtain a description of the physical setting, a description of the events immediately preceding the role play, a description of the manner the co-actor should display, and any other information that would increase realism.

It is crucial that the main actor use the behavioral steps that have been modeled. This is the main purpose of the role playing. Before beginning the actual role playing, the trainer should go over each step as it applies to the particular role-play situation, thus preparing the main actor to make a successful effort. The main actor is told to refer to the Skill Card on which the behavioral steps are printed. As noted previously, the behavioral steps are written on a chalkboard visible to the main actor as well as the rest of the group during the role playing. Before the role playing begins, trainers should remind all of the participants of their roles and responsibilities: the main actor is told to follow the behavioral steps; the co-actor, to stay in the role of the other person; and the observers, to watch carefully for the enactment of the behavioral steps. At times, feedback from other trainees is facilitated by assigning each one a single behavioral step to focus upon and provide feedback on after the role play. For the first several role plays, the observers also can be coached on kinds of cues (posture, tone of voice, content of speech, etc.) to observe.

During the role play, it is the responsibility of one of the trainers to provide the main actor with whatever help, coaching, and encouragement she needs to keep the role playing going according to the behavioral steps. Trainees who "break role" and begin to explain their behavior or make observer-like comments should be urged to get back into the role and explain later. If the role play is clearly going astray from the behavioral steps, the scene can be stopped, needed instruction can be provided, and then the role play can be restarted. One trainer should be positioned near the chalkboard in order to point to each of the behavioral steps in turn as the role play unfolds, thus helping the main actor (as well as the other trainees) to follow each of the steps in order. The second trainer should sit with the observing trainees to be available as needed to keep them on task.

The role playing should be continued until all trainees have had an opportunity to participate in the role of main actor. Sometimes this will require two or three sessions for a given skill. As we suggested before, each session should begin with two new modeling vignettes for the chosen skill, even if the skill is not new to the group. It is important to note once again that while the framework (behavioral steps) of each role play in the series remains the same, the actual content can and should change from role play to role play. It is the problem as it actually occurs, or could occur, in each trainee's real-life environment that should be the content of the given role play.

There are a few more ways to increase the effectiveness of role playing. Role reversal is often a useful role-play procedure. A trainee role playing a skill may on occasion have a difficult time perceiving her co-actor's viewpoint and vice versa. Having them exchange roles and resume the role play can be most helpful in this regard. At times, the trainer can also assume the co-actor role in an effort to give the trainee the opportunity to handle types of reactions not otherwise role played during the session. For example, it may be crucial to have a difficult co-actor realistically portrayed. The trainer as co-actor may also be particularly helpful when dealing with less verbal or more hesitant trainees.

PERFORMANCE FEEDBACK

A brief feedback period follows each role play. This helps the main actor find out how well she followed or departed from the behavioral steps. It also examines the psychological impact of the enactment on the co-actor, and provides the main actor with encouragement to try out the role-played behaviors in real life. The trainer should ask the main actor to wait until she has heard everyone's comments before responding to them.

The co-actor is asked about his reactions first. Next the observers comment on how well the behavioral steps were followed and other relevant aspects of the role play. Then the trainers comment in particular on how well the behavioral steps were followed and provide social reinforcement (praise, approval, encouragement) for close following. To be most effective in their use of reinforcement, trainers should follow these guidelines:

1. Provide reinforcement only after role plays that follow the behavioral steps.
2. Provide reinforcement at the earliest appropriate opportunity after role plays that follow the behavioral steps.
3. Vary the specific content of the reinforcements offered, for example, praise particular aspects of the performance, such as tone of voice, posture, phrasing, etc.
4. Provide enough role-playing activity for each group member to have sufficient opportunity to be reinforced.
5. Provide reinforcement in an amount consistent with the quality of the given role play.
6. Provide no reinforcement when the role play departs significantly from the behavioral steps (except for "trying" in the first session or two).
7. Provide reinforcement for an individual trainee's improvement over previous performances.
8. Always provide reinforcement to the co-actor for being helpful, cooperative, etc.

In all aspects of feedback, it is crucial that the trainer maintain the behavioral focus of Structured Learning. Both trainer and trainee comments should point to the presence or absence of specific, concrete behaviors and not take the form of general evaluations or broad generalities. Feedback, of course, may be positive or negative in content. Negative comments should always be followed by a constructive comment as to how a particular fault might be improved. At minimum, a "poor" performance can be praised as "a good try" at the same time that it is being criticized for its real faults. If at all possible, trainees failing to follow the relevant behavioral steps in their role play should be given the opportunity to role play these same behavioral steps again after receiving corrective feedback. At times, as a further feedback procedure, we have audio- or videotaped entire role plays. Giving trainees post-role-play opportunities to observe themselves on tape can be an effective aid, enabling them to reflect on their own verbal and nonverbal behavior and its impact upon others.

Since a primary goal of Structured Learning is skill flexibility, role play enactments that depart somewhat from the behavioral steps may not be "wrong." That is, a different approach to the skill may in fact work in some situations. Trainers should stress that they are trying to teach effective alternatives and that the trainees would do well to have the behavioral steps being taught, or as collaboratively modified, in their repertoire of skill behaviors, available when needed.

TRANSFER TRAINING

Several aspects of the training sessions already described have been designed primarily to make it likely that learning in the training setting will transfer to the trainees' actual real-life environments. Techniques for enhancing transfer training that are used in the training sessions follow.

Provision of General Principles

It has been demonstrated that transfer of training is facilitated by providing trainees with some general mediating principles governing successful or competent performance in both the training and applied real-world settings. This has been operationalized in laboratory contexts by providing subjects with the organizing concepts, principles, strategies, or rationales that explain the stimulus-response relationships operating in both the training and application settings. General principles of skill selection and utilization are provided to Structured Learning trainees verbally, visually, and in written form.

Overlearning

Overlearning involves training in a skill beyond what is necessary to produce initial changes in behavior. The overlearning, or repetition of successful skill enactment, in the typical Structured Learning session is quite substantial. Each of the skills taught and its behavioral steps are:

1. Modeled several times,
2. Role played one or more times by the trainee,
3. Observed live by the trainee as every other group member role plays,
4. Read by the trainee from a chalkboard and a Skill Card,
5. Practiced in real-life settings one or more times by the trainee as part of his formal homework assignment.

Identical Elements

In perhaps the earliest research on transfer enhancement, Thorndike and Woodworth (1901) concluded that when one habit encouraged another, it was to the extent that they shared identical elements. More recently, Ellis (1965) and Osgood (1953) have emphasized the importance for transfer of similarity between stimulus aspects of the training and application tasks. The greater the similarity of physical and interpersonal stimuli in the Structured Learning setting and the homework and community or other setting in which the skill is to be applied, the greater the likelihood of transfer. Structured Learning is made similar to real life in several ways. These include:

1. Designing the live modeling displays to be highly similar to what trainees face in their daily lives through the representative, relevant, and realistic portrayal of the models, protagonists, and situations;
2. Designing the role plays to be similar to real-life situations through the use of props, the physical arrangement of the setting, and the choice of realistic co-actors;
3. Conducting the role play to be as responsive as possible to the real-life interpersonal stimuli to which the trainees must actually respond later with the given skill;
4. Rehearsing of each skill in role plays as the trainees actually plan to use it;
5. Assigning of homework.

Stimulus Variability

Positive transfer is greater when a variety of relevant training stimuli are employed (Callantine & Warren, 1955; Duncan, 1958; Shore & Sechrest, 1961). This important element of stimulus variability may be implemented in Structured Learning sessions by use of the following activities:

1. Rotation of group leaders across groups,
2. Rotation of trainees across groups,
3. Role playing of a given skill by trainees with several different co-actors,
4. Role playing of a given skill by trainees across several relevant settings,
5. Completion of multiple homework assignments for each given skill.

Real-life Reinforcement

Given successful implementation of both appropriate Structured Learning procedures and the transfer enhancement procedures, positive transfer may still fail to occur. As Agras (1967), Gruber (1971), Patterson and Anderson (1964), Tharp and Wetzel (1969), and dozens of other investigators have shown, stable and enduring performance in application settings of newly learned skills is very much at the mercy of real-life reinforcement contingencies. We have found it useful to implement several supplemental programs outside of the Structured Learning setting that can help to provide the rewards trainees need to maintain new behaviors. These programs include provision for both external social rewards (provided by people in the trainees' real-life environments) and self-rewards (provided by the trainees themselves). A particularly useful tool for transfer enhancement, a tool combining the possibilities of identical elements, stimulus variability, and real-life reinforcement, is the skill homework assignment.

When possible, we urge use of a homework technique we have found to be successful with most groups. In this procedure, trainees are instructed to try in their own real-life settings the behaviors they have practiced during the session. The name of the person(s) with whom they will try it, the day, the place, etc., are all discussed. The trainee is urged to take notes on his attempt to use the skill on the

Homework Report form (page 73). This form requests detailed information about what happened when the trainee attempted the homework assignment, how well he followed the relevant behavioral steps, the trainee's evaluation of his performance, and thoughts about what the next assignment might appropriately be.

It has often proven useful to start with relatively simple homework behaviors and, as mastery is achieved, work up to more complex and demanding assignments. This provides both the trainer and the people who are the targets of the homework with an opportunity to reinforce each approximation of the more complex target behavior. Successful experiences at beginning homework attempts are crucial in encouraging the trainee to further attempt real-life skill use.

The first part of each Structured Learning session is devoted to presenting and discussing these homework reports. When trainees have made an effort to complete their homework assignments, trainers should provide social reinforcement, while failure to do homework should be met with some chagrin and expressed disappointment, followed by support and encouragement to complete the assignment. It cannot be stressed too strongly that without these or similar attempts to maximize transfer, the value of the entire training effort is in severe jeopardy.

LATER SESSIONS

Much of the foregoing procedural material may be conveniently summarized for purposes of review by the following outline.

Outline of Later Session Procedures

A. Homework review.
B. Trainer presents overview of the skill.
    1. Introduces skill briefly prior to showing modeling display.
    2. Asks questions that will help trainees define the skill in their own language.
        Examples:—"Who knows what _____ is?"
                —"What does _____ mean to you?"
                —"Who can define _____?"
    3. Postpones lengthier discussion until after trainees view the modeling display. If trainees want to engage in further discussion, the trainer might say, "Let's wait until after we've seen some examples of people using the skill before we talk about it in more detail."
    4. Makes a statement about what will follow the modeling display.

Example:—"After we see the examples, we will talk about times
when you've had to use ＿＿＿＿ and times when
you may have to use that skill in the future."
5. Distributes Skill Cards, asking a trainee to read the behavioral steps aloud.
6. Asks trainees to follow each step in the modeling display as the step is depicted.
C. Trainer presents modeling display.
1. Provides two relevant examples of the skill in use, following its behavioral steps.
D. Trainer invites discussion of skill that has been modeled.
1. Invites comments on how the situation modeled may remind trainees of situations involving skill usage in their own lives.
Example:—"Did any of the situations you just saw remind you of times when you have had to ＿＿＿＿?"
2. Asks questions that encourage trainees to talk about skill usage and problems involving skill usage.
Examples:—"What do you do in situations where you have to ＿＿＿＿?"
—"Have you ever had to ＿＿＿＿?"
—"Have you ever had difficulty ＿＿＿＿?"
E. Trainer organizes role play.
1. Asks a trainee who has volunteered a situation to elaborate on his remarks, obtaining details on where, when, and with whom the skill might be useful in the future.
2. Designates this trainee as a main actor, and asks the trainee to choose a co-actor (someone who reminds the main actor of the person with whom the skill will be used in the real-life situation).
Examples:—"What does ＿＿＿＿ look like?"
—"Who in the group reminds you of ＿＿＿＿ in some way?"
3. Gets additional information from the main actor, if necessary, and sets the stage for the role playing (including props, furniture arrangement, etc.).
Examples:—"Where might you be talking to ＿＿＿＿?"
—"How is the room furnished?"
—"Would you be standing or sitting?"
—"What time of day will it be?"
4. Rehearses with the main actor what he will say and do during the role play.
Examples:—"What will you say for Step 1 of the skill?"
—"What will you do if the co-actor does ＿＿＿＿?"
5. Gives each group member some final instructions as to his part just prior to role playing.

Examples:—To the main actor: "Try to follow all of the steps as best you can."
—To the co-actor: "Try to play the part of _____ as best you can. Say and do what you think _____ would do when _____ follows the skill's steps."
—To the other trainees in the group: "Watch how well _____ follows the steps so that we can talk about it after the role play."

F. Trainer instructs the role players to begin.
1. One trainer stands at the chalkboard and points to each step as it is enacted and provides whatever coaching or prompting is needed by the main actor or co-actor.
2. The other trainer sits with the observing trainees to help keep them attending to the unfolding role play.
3. In the event that the role play strays markedly from the behavioral steps, the trainers stop the scene, provide needed instruction, and begin again.

G. Trainer invites feedback following role play.
1. Asks the main actor to wait until he has heard everyone's comments before talking.
2. Asks the co-actor, "In the role of _____, how did _____ make you feel? What were your reactions to him?"
3. Asks observing trainees: "How well were the behavioral steps followed?" "What specific things did you like or dislike?" "In what ways did the co-actor do a good job?"
4. Comments on the following of the behavioral steps, provides social reward, points out what was done well, and comments on what else might be done to make the enactment even better.
5. Asks main actor: "Now that you have heard everyone's comments, how do you feel about the job you did?" "How do you think that following the steps worked out?"

H. Trainer helps role player to plan homework.
1. Asks the main actor how, when, and with whom he might attempt the behavioral steps prior to the next class meeting.
2. As appropriate, the Homework Report may be used to get a written commitment from the main actor to try out his new skill and report back to the group at the next meeting.
3. Trainees who have not had a chance to role play during a particular class may also be assigned homework in the form of looking for situations relevant to the skill that they might role play during the next class meeting.

Homework Report

Name: _____   Date: _____

Group Leaders: _____

Fill in During This Group Meeting:

1. What skill will you use?

2. What are the steps for the skill?

3. Where will you try the skill?

4. With whom will you try the skill?

5. When will you try the skill?

Fill in After Doing Your Homework:

1. What happened when you did the homework?

2. Which steps did you really follow?

3. How good a job did you do in using the skill? (Circle one.)

    Excellent   Good   Fair   Poor

4. What do you think should be your next homework assignment?

Chapter Six

Structured Learning Skills for Abusive Parents

In the previous chapters we have presented how Structured Learning groups are planned, organized, and conducted. Now we wish to turn away from concern with how skills are taught and focus instead on the specific Structured Learning curriculum. We have developed 24 Structured Learning skills, falling into four content areas, especially relevant to the needs of abusive parents. These skills come from a number of sources. Some derive from our extensive examination of diverse educational and psychological studies yielding information on which behaviors constitute successful self-control, parenting, marital, and general interpersonal functioning in a variety of settings. Our own direct observation of abusive parents in various agency and real-life settings is a second source. Many Structured Learning groups have been conducted by us and by others. Trainers and trainees in these groups have been a particularly valuable source of skill-relevant information.

This chapter includes the behavioral steps that constitute each skill. These steps are the framework for the vignettes or stories that are modeled by trainers and then role played by trainees. In addition to the Structured Learning Core Skills, we have also developed and regularly taught a number of additional Structured Learning skills created originally for other types of adult (Goldstein et al., 1976) and adolescent (Goldstein et al., 1980) trainees. These 13 supplementary skills are presented after the core skills. Supplementary skills, when selected by trainers and/or trainees as the group's target skill, should be taught using the same procedures as used for the core skills.

For each skill in the curriculum, we provide in the pages that follow the behavioral steps that constitute the skill, trainer notes that facilitate the effective role playing of each skill, and a blank Notes section in which the user may record aids or tips of his own that appear to facilitate instruction of the given skill. The 24 core skills and the 13 supplementary skills are listed in Table 1 in the order in which they are presented in this chapter.

Table 1. Structured Learning Skills for Abusive Parents

Group I.   *Self-control Skills*
    1. Identifying and Labeling Your Emotions
    2. Relaxing
    3. Using Self-control
    4. Concentrating on a Task
    5. Deciding What Caused a Problem
    6. Setting Problem Priorities

Group II.   *Parenting Skills*
    7. Expressing Anger
    8. Expressing Affection
    9. Evaluating Your Abilities
    10. Making a Decision
    11. Setting a Goal
    12. Helping Others

Group III.   *Marital Skills*
    13. Responding to the Feelings of Others
    14. Responding to a Complaint
    15. Responding to Anger
    16. Responding to Contradictory Messages
    17. Preparing for a Stressful Conversation
    18. Negotiating

Group IV.   *Interpersonal Skills*
    19. Starting a Conversation
    20. Expressing Appreciation
    21. Asking for Help
    22. Giving Instructions
    23. Being Assertive
    24. Responding to Failure

Group V. Supplementary Skills
   25. Listening
   26. Asking a Question
   27. Giving a Compliment
   28. Giving Encouragement
   29. Making a Complaint
   30. Persuading Others
   31. Responding to Praise
   32. Apologizing
   33. Following Instructions
   34. Responding to Persuasion
   35. Dealing with Embarrassment
   36. Dealing with an Accusation
   37. Dealing with Group Pressure

GROUP I. SELF-CONTROL SKILLS

Skill 1. Identifying and Labeling Your Emotions

STEPS	TRAINER NOTES
1. Pay attention to those body signals that help you know what you are feeling.	Some cues are blushing, butterflies in your stomach, tight muscles, etc.
2. Decide which outside events may have caused you to have these feelings.	Focus on outside events such as a fight, a surprise, etc.
3. Consider all of this information and decide what you are feeling.	Possibilities are anger, fear, embarrassment, joy, happiness, sadness, disappointment, frustration, excitement, anxiety, etc. Trainer should place a list of feelings on the board and encourage trainees to contribute additional suggestions.

NOTES:

GROUP I. SELF-CONTROL SKILLS

Skill 2. Relaxing

STEPS	TRAINER NOTES
1. Pay attention to those body signals that help you know you are tense.	Some cues are tightened muscles, clenched fists, and rapid breathing.
2. Decide whether you would like to relax.	
3. Tell yourself to calm down and relax.	Do this step out loud at first, in a whisper in later role plays, and eventually silently in actual use.
4. Imagine the scene that you find most calm and peaceful.	Try as best as you can to imagine yourself actually being there.
5. Pay attention to those body signals that help you know you are relaxed.	Some cues are loosened muscles and slower and deeper breathing.

NOTES:

GROUP I. SELF-CONTROL SKILLS

Skill 3. Using Self-control

STEPS	TRAINER NOTES
1. Pay attention to those body signals that help you know you are about to lose control of yourself.	Are you getting tense, angry, hot, fidgety?
2. Decide which events may have caused you to feel frustrated.	Consider both outside events and "internal" events (thoughts).
3. Consider ways in which you might control yourself.	Slow down; count to 10; breathe deeply; assert yourself; leave; do something else.
4. Choose the most effective way of controlling yourself and do it.	

NOTES:

GROUP I. SELF-CONTROL SKILLS

Skill 4. Concentrating on a Task

STEPS	TRAINER NOTES
1. Set a realistic goal.	See Skill 11.
2. Decide on a reasonable time schedule.	Consider when and how long to work.
3. Gather the materials you need.	
4. Arrange your surroundings to minimize distraction.	Consider where to work; noise level; people present or anticipated; possible interruptions.
5. Judge whether your preparation is complete and begin the task.	

NOTES:

GROUP I. SELF-CONTROL SKILLS

Skill 5. Deciding What Caused a Problem

STEPS	TRAINER NOTES
1. Decide what the problem is.	
2. Consider possible causes of the problem.	Was it yourself, others, events, intentional actions, accidental actions, or a combination?
3. Decide which are the most likely causes of the problem.	Consider past experiences and the experiences of others.
4. Take actions to test out which are the actual causes of the problem.	Ask others; observe the situation again.

NOTES:

GROUP I. SELF-CONTROL SKILLS

Skill 6. Setting Problem Priorities

STEPS	TRAINER NOTES
1. List all of the problems that are currently pressuring you.	Make a list; be inclusive.
2. Arrange this list in order, from most to least urgent problem.	
3. Take steps to decrease temporarily the urgency of all but the most pressing problem.	Delegate them; postpone them; avoid them.
4. Concentrate on dealing with the most pressing problem.	Plan first steps in dealing with the most important problem; rehearse these steps in your imagination.

NOTES:

GROUP II. PARENTING SKILLS

Skill 7. Expressing Anger

STEPS	TRAINER NOTES
1. Pay attention to those body signals that help you know what you are feeling.	Some cues are tight muscles, flushed skin, feeling hot, restlessness, and pacing.
2. Decide which events may have caused you to have these feelings.	Consider both internal triggers (thoughts) and outside triggers (events, behavior of others).
3. Decide if you are feeling angry about these events.	
4. Decide how you can best express these angry feelings.	Confront; ignore; postpone; meet face-to-face; telephone; get help from others; etc.
5. Express your angry feelings in a direct and honest manner.	

NOTES:

GROUP II. PARENTING SKILLS

Skill 8. Expressing Affection

STEPS	TRAINER NOTES
1. Decide if you have warm, caring feelings about the other person.	
2. Decide whether the other person would like to know about your feelings.	Consider the possible consequences, such as happiness, misinterpretation, embarrassment, encouragement of friendship, etc.
3. Decide how you might best express your feelings.	Do something; say something; give a gift; telephone; send a card; extend an invitation; etc.
4. Choose the right time and place to express your feelings.	Minimize distractions and possible interruptions.
5. Express affection in a warm and caring manner.	

NOTES:

GROUP II. PARENTING SKILLS

Skill 9. Evaluating Your Abilities

STEPS	TRAINER NOTES
1. Decide which ability you need to evaluate.	Take the setting, circumstances, and goal into account.
2. Think about how you have done in the past when you have tried to use this ability.	
3. Get any outside information you can about your ability.	Ask others; take tests; check records.
4. Use all of this evidence and realistically evaluate your ability.	Consider the evidence from both Steps 2 and 3.

NOTES:

GROUP II. PARENTING SKILLS

Skill 10. Making a Decision

STEPS	TRAINER NOTES
1. Gather accurate information needed to make the decision.	Ask others; read; observe.
2. Evaluate the information in light of your goal.	Generate a number of possible alternatives; avoid premature closure.
3. Make a decision which is in both your best interest and the interests of others.	

NOTES:

GROUP II. PARENTING SKILLS

Skill 11. Setting a Goal

STEPS	TRAINER NOTES
1. Decide what you would like to accomplish.	
2. Decide what you would need to do to reach this hoped-for goal.	Talk with friends; read; observe others; ask authorities; etc.
3. Decide on the order in which you would do these things.	
4. Judge whether your planning is realistic.	Consider your abilities, materials and skills needed, the help available from others, etc.
5. Set a realistic goal.	

NOTES:

GROUP II. PARENTING SKILLS

Skill 12. Helping Others

STEPS	TRAINER NOTES
1. Decide if the other person might need and want your help.	Think about the needs of the other person; observe the situation.
2. Think of the ways you could be helpful.	Do something; give encouragement; get help from someone else; etc.
3. Ask the other person if he/she needs and wants your help.	Make the offer sincere, allowing the other person to decline if he/she wishes.
4. Help the other person.	

NOTES:

GROUP III. MARITAL SKILLS

Skill 13. Responding to the Feelings of Others

STEPS	TRAINER NOTES
1. Watch the other person.	Notice tone of voice, posture, and facial expression.
2. Listen to what the person is saying.	Try to understand the content.
3. Figure out what the other person might be feeling.	He/she may be angry, sad, anxious, etc.
4. Think about ways to show that you understand what he/she is feeling.	You might tell the person, touch him/her, or leave the person alone.
5. Decide on the best way and do it.	

NOTES:

GROUP III. MARITAL SKILLS

Skill 14. Responding to a Complaint

STEPS	TRAINER NOTES
1. Listen openly to the complaint.	
2. Ask the person to explain anything you don't understand.	
3. Show that you understand the other person's thoughts and feelings.	Rephrase; acknowledge the content and feeling.
4. Tell the other person your thoughts and feelings, accepting responsibility if appropriate.	
5. Suggest what each of you could do about the complaint.	Compromise; defend your position; apologize; etc.

NOTES:

GROUP III. MARITAL SKILLS

Skill 15. Responding to Anger

STEPS	TRAINER NOTES
1. Listen to the person who is angry.	Don't interrupt; stay calm.
2. Try to understand what the angry person is saying and feeling.	Ask questions to get explanations of what you don't understand, restate the explanations to yourself and, if appropriate, to the other person.
3. Decide if you can say or do something to deal with the situation.	Think about ways of dealing with the problem. This may include just listening, being empathic, doing something to correct the problem, ignoring it, or being assertive.
4. If you can, deal with the other person's anger.	

NOTES:

GROUP III. MARITAL SKILLS

Skill 16. Responding to Contradictory Messages

STEPS	TRAINER NOTES
1. Pay attention to those body signals that help you know you are feeling trapped or confused.	Some cues are tight muscles, flushed face, feeling warm or hot, and other sensations of anxiety or anger.
2. Pay attention to the other person's words and actions that may have caused you to have these feelings.	
3. Decide whether his/her words and actions are contradictory.	Are they consistent or inconsistent? Is the person saying one thing but doing the opposite?
4. Decide whether it would be useful to point out the contradiction.	
5. Ask the other person to explain the contradiction.	

NOTES:

GROUP III. MARITAL SKILLS

Skill 17. Preparing for a Stressful Conversation

STEPS	TRAINER NOTES
1. Think about how you will feel during the conversation.	You might be tense, anxious, or impatient.
2. Think about how the other person will feel.	He/she may feel anxious, bored, angry, or afraid.
3. Think about different ways you could say what you want to say.	
4. Think about what the other person might say back to you.	
5. Think about any other things that might happen during the conversation.	Repeat Steps 1-5 at least twice, using different approaches to the situation.
6. Choose the best approach you can think of and try it.	

NOTES:

GROUP III. MARITAL SKILLS

Skill 18. Negotiating

STEPS	TRAINER NOTES
1. State your position.	Be as clear and factual as you can.
2. State your understanding of the other person's position.	Try to see the problem as he/she sees it.
3. Ask if the other person agrees with your statement of his/her position.	
4. Listen openly to the other person's response.	
5. Propose a compromise.	Fairly take into account the opinions and feelings of both yourself and the other person.

NOTES:

GROUP IV. INTERPERSONAL SKILLS

Skill 19. Starting a Conversation

STEPS	TRAINER NOTES
1. Choose the right place and time.	Choose a place and time where and when you expect a minimum of interruptions or distractions and the most interest and attention from the other person.
2. Greet the other person.	Say "hello"; shake hands; etc.
3. Make small talk.	Discuss the weather, sports, clothing, or a recent event.
4. Judge if the other person is listening and wants to talk with you.	Is he/she looking at you, nodding, or saying "mm-hmm"?
5. Open the main topic you want to talk about.	

NOTES:

GROUP IV. INTERPERSONAL SKILLS

Skill 20. Expressing Appreciation

STEPS	TRAINER NOTES
1. Clearly describe to the other person *what* he/she did for you that deserves appreciation.	It may have been a favor, gift, etc.
2. Tell the other person *why* you appreciate what he/she did.	
3. Ask the other person if there is anything you can do for him/her.	

NOTES:

GROUP IV. INTERPERSONAL SKILLS

Skill 21. Asking for Help

STEPS	TRAINER NOTES
1. Decide what the problem is.	Be specific; who and what are contributing to the problem; what is its effect on you.
2. Decide if you want help for the problem.	Figure out if you can solve the problem alone.
3. Think about different people who might help you and pick one.	Consider all possible helpers and choose the best one.
4. Tell the person about the problem and ask that person to help you.	

NOTES:

GROUP IV. INTERPERSONAL SKILLS

Skill 22. Giving Instructions

STEPS	TRAINER NOTES
1. Define what needs to be done and who should do it.	Think about all of the people who might reasonably do it before choosing one.
2. Tell the other person what you want him/her to do and why.	
3. Tell the other person exactly how he/she is to do what you want.	Be specific, especially if the task is complex.
4. Ask for his/her reactions.	
5. Consider his/her reactions and change your directions to him/her if appropriate.	

NOTES:

GROUP IV. INTERPERSONAL SKILLS

Skill 23. Being Assertive

STEPS	TRAINER NOTES
1. Pay attention to what is going on in your body that helps you know that you are dissatisfied and would like to stand up for yourself.	Some cues are tight muscles, butterflies in your stomach, and feeling restless.
2. Decide what happened to make you feel dissatisfied.	Are you being taken advantage of, ignored, mistreated, or teased?
3. Think about ways in which you might stand up for yourself and choose one.	Seek help; say what is on your mind; get a majority opinion; choose the right time and place.
4. Stand up for yourself in a direct and reasonable way.	

NOTES:

76960

GROUP IV. INTERPERSONAL SKILLS

Skill 24. Responding to Failure

STEPS	TRAINER NOTES
1. Decide if you have failed at something.	The failure may involve self-control, parenting, or interpersonal behavior.
2. Think about why you failed.	It could be due to skill, motivation, or luck. Include personal reasons and circumstances.
3. Think about what you could do to keep from failing another time.	Evaluate what is under your control to change: if a skill problem—practice; if motivation—increase effort; if circumstances—think of ways to change them.
4. Decide if you want to try again.	
5. Try again using your new idea.	

NOTES:

GROUP V. SUPPLEMENTARY SKILLS

Skill 25. Listening

STEPS	TRAINER NOTES
1. Look at the person who is speaking.	Face the person; establish eye contact.
2. Show your interest in the other's statement.	Show this by nodding your head, saying "mm-hmm."
3. Ask questions on the same topic.	
4. Add your thoughts and feelings on the topic.	

NOTES:

GROUP V. SUPPLEMENTARY SKILLS

Skill 26. Asking a Question

STEPS	TRAINER NOTES
1. Decide what you'd like to know more about.	Ask about something you don't understand, something you didn't hear, or something confusing.
2. Decide whom to ask.	Think about who has the best information on a topic; consider asking several people.
3. Think about different ways to ask your question and pick one way.	Think about wording; ask nonchallengingly.
4. Pick the right time and place to ask your question.	Wait for a pause; wait for privacy.
5. Ask your question.	

NOTES:

GROUP V. SUPPLEMENTARY SKILLS

Skill 27. Giving a Compliment

STEPS	TRAINER NOTES
1. Decide what you want to compliment about the other person.	It may be his/her appearance, behavior, or an accomplishment.
2. Decide how to give the compliment.	Consider the wording and ways to keep the other person and yourself from feeling embarrassed.
3. Choose the right time and place to say it.	It may be a private place or a time when the other person is unoccupied.
4. Give the compliment.	Be friendly and sincere.

NOTES:

GROUP V. SUPPLEMENTARY SKILLS

Skill 28. Giving Encouragement

STEPS	TRAINER NOTES
1. Ask the other person how he/she feels about the way he/she is handling the situation.	This information is useful in deciding Step 2.
2. Decide if it might be helpful to encourage the other person.	
3. Decide what type of encouragement might be most helpful to the other person.	Reassurance; reminder of past performance; facts about the current situation; being with the other person; etc.
4. Express encouragement in a sincere and friendly manner.	

NOTES:

GROUP V. SUPPLEMENTARY SKILLS

Skill 29. Making a Complaint

STEPS	TRAINER NOTES
1. Decide what your complaint is.	What is the problem?
2. Decide who to complain to.	Who can resolve it?
3. Tell that person your complaint.	Consider alternative ways to complain, such as politely, assertively, or privately.
4. Tell that person what you would like done about the problem.	Offer a helpful suggestion about resolving the problem.
5. Ask how he/she feels about what you've said.	

NOTES:

GROUP V. SUPPLEMENTARY SKILLS

Skill 30. Persuading Others

STEPS	TRAINER NOTES
1. Decide on your position and what the other person's is likely to be.	It might be doing something your way, going someplace, interpreting events, or evaluating ideas.
2. State your position clearly, completely, and in a way that is acceptable to the other person.	Focus on both ideas and feelings.
3. State what you think is the other person's position.	Try your best to be fair; "get in the other person's shoes."
4. Restate your position, emphasizing why it is the better of the two.	Stress facts; take the other person's position into account.
5. Suggest that the other person consider your position for a while before making a decision.	

NOTES:

GROUP V. SUPPLEMENTARY SKILLS

Skill 31. Responding to Praise

STEPS	TRAINER NOTES
1. Listen openly to the other person's statement of praise.	
2. Tell the other person how his/her statement makes you feel.	
3. Thank the other person in a warm and sincere manner.	

NOTES:

GROUP V. SUPPLEMENTARY SKILLS

Skill 32. Apologizing

STEPS	TRAINER NOTES
1. Decide if it would be best for you to apologize for something you did.	You might apologize for breaking something, making an error, interrupting someone, hurting someone's feelings, etc.
2. Think of the different ways you could apologize.	Say something; do something; write something.
3. Choose the best time and place to apologize.	Do it privately and as quickly as possible after creating the problem.
4. Make your apology.	This might include an offer to make up for what happened.

NOTES:

GROUP V. SUPPLEMENTARY SKILLS

Skill 33. Following Instructions

STEPS	TRAINER NOTES
1. Listen carefully while the instructions are being given.	Take notes if necessary; nod your head; say "mm-hmm."
2. Ask questions about anything you don't understand.	The goal is making instructions more specific, more clear.
3. Decide if you want to follow the instructions and let the other person know your decision.	
4. Repeat the instructions to yourself.	Do this in your own words.
5. Imagine yourself following the instructions and then do it.	

NOTES:

GROUP V. SUPPLEMENTARY SKILLS

Skill 34. Responding to Persuasion

STEPS	TRAINER NOTES
1. Listen to the other person's ideas on the topic.	Listen openly; try to see the topic from the other person's viewpoint.
2. Decide what you think about the topic.	Distinguish your own ideas from the ideas of others.
3. Compare what he/she said with what you think.	Consider the pros and cons of both sides.
4. Decide which idea you like better and tell the other person about it.	Agree; disagree; modify your position; postpone a decision.

NOTES:

GROUP V. SUPPLEMENTARY SKILLS

Skill 35. Dealing with Embarrassment

STEPS	TRAINER NOTES
1. Decide if you are feeling embarrassed.	
2. Decide what happened to make you feel embarrassed.	
3. Decide on what will help you feel less embarrassed and do it.	Correct the cause; minimize it; ignore it; distract others; use humor; reassure yourself.

NOTES:

GROUP V. SUPPLEMENTARY SKILLS

Skill 36. Dealing with an Accusation

STEPS	TRAINER NOTES
1. Think about what the other person has accused you of.	Is the accusation accurate or inaccurate? Was it said in a mean way or a constructive way?
2. Think about why the person might have accused you.	Have you infringed on his/her rights or property?
3. Think about ways to answer the person's accusation.	Deny it; explain your own behavior; correct the other person's perceptions; assert yourself; apologize; offer to make up for what happened.
4. Choose the best way and do it.	

NOTES:

GROUP V. SUPPLEMENTARY SKILLS

Skill 37. Dealing with Group Pressure

STEPS	TRAINER NOTES
1. Think about what the group wants you to do and why.	Listen to other people; decide what the real meaning is; try to understand what is being said.
2. Decide what you want to do.	Yield; resist; delay; negotiate.
3. Decide how to tell the group what you want to do.	Give reasons; talk to one person only; delay; assert yourself.
4. Tell the group what you have decided.	

NOTES:

Chapter Seven

A Typical
Structured Learning Session

This chapter presents an edited transcript of an excerpt from a Structured Learning session with eight abusive parents. The skill being taught is Using Self-control (Skill 3). The transcript reports the sequence for teaching Structured Learning skills as listed in the Outline for Later Sessions (Chapter Five), that is, skill introduction and overview, modeling, discussion of the model, organization of the role play, the role play itself, performance feedback, and assignment of homework. The reader should view this chapter itself as a modeling display for trainers, illustrating in concrete detail how we believe a Structured Learning session should be conducted.

INTRODUCTION AND OVERVIEW OF THE SKILL

Trainer: Okay, today's skill is using self-control. Let's talk about it a little bit before we see the modeling tape. Self-control has just four steps to it. While I'm describing them, you can pass around these Skill Cards with the four steps on them. The first has to do with tuning in to, or paying attention to, what is going on in your body that lets you know that you are about to lose control of yourself. Your muscles may feel tight, the hair on your neck may be standing up, you may feel flushed, and you know that you are getting angry and something is about to pop. The second behavioral step is to decide what outside events have caused you to feel this way—frustrated, ready to pop. Maybe someone said or did something, perhaps your child didn't want to quiet down, or maybe the landlord is demanding the rent. These are examples of outside events. Inside events are making you feel this way too, like the things you say to yourself when these things happen. The third behavioral step is to think about ways you might control yourself. There are several different ways: breathing deeply, relaxing, counting to 10, ignoring it, walking away, or talking to the person that's causing you to feel this way. Think about which of these alternatives might work best for you. Finally, for the fourth step, choose the way you think would be most effective and do it. If you go through these four steps, you've used self-control. And that's what we're here to learn today. The way we're going to do it is the way we usually do it. I'm going to show you now on the videotape people using these four steps, then we'll talk about it briefly and have each of you get up and practice. Okay? Are we together? Good. Okay, I'm going to put this on now. Please pay attention to the tape.

PRESENTATION OF THE MODELING DISPLAY

Vignette 1

Narrator: Behavioral steps:
Step 1. Pay attention to those body signals that help you know you are about to lose control of yourself.
Step 2. Decide which events may have caused you to feel frustrated.
Step 3. Consider ways in which you might control yourself.
Step 4. Choose the most effective way of controlling yourself and do it.

Actor I: **[Step 1.]** This party is really getting me uptight. My jaw is starting to hurt. My neck is giving me a headache.
[Step 2.] It's John's friends and John's party. All I get out of it is work, work, work. Do the shopping, fix the food, clean the house, bathe the kids, get myself ready. Boy, would I love to dump this mop water over his party-planning head.
[Step 3.] I'd better watch it. Better calm down before I do or say something I'll regret. What I really need is help. Maybe if I ask John in a nice way, he'll give me a hand.
[Step 4.] That really is the best way. With help, I'll have time to relax in a hot tub before the party.

Actor II: Hi, hon. How are plans for the party coming?

Actor I: Well, I really knew it would be hard. I really could use some help. If I made the shopping lists, do you think you could do the shopping for me?

Actor II: Sure. I'll do that later this afternoon before the party.

Actor I: Good.

Vignette 2

Actor III: Mrs. Kane, I can't believe you haven't brought those three little ones in for their regular checkups and shots. Don't you know how important those medical appointments are? Oh, I have to see someone for a minute. I'll be right back. Excuse me, please.

Actor IV: **[Step 1.]** All this crowding. She makes me sick. I really feel sick and tense all over. I feel like walking out of here.

[Step 2.] She's been very angry with me. You know, she just doesn't realize how hard it is with three kids to get on a bus, get to a clinic, and sit there and wait for hours.

[Step 3.] Just take it easy now. I could take a few deep breaths or just try to ignore her. Sometimes it even helps me to think of being at a quiet place, like down at the lake.

[Step 4.] Yeah, that's what I'll do, think of the lake. I can feel myself getting a little cooler already.

DISCUSSION OF MODELED SKILL

Trainer: Okay. These are two examples of using self-control. We all have difficulty with self-control some of the time. What about you folks? What would be an example of losing self-control that has happened to you? George, have you got one in mind? You seem to be thinking about it.

George: Yeah. I think I've had that problem.

Trainer: Could you tell us a little about it?

George: Well, I lost it a little bit but I gained it back after a day or a day and a half.

Trainer: You got angry at somebody?

George: You could say that; I got very angry; I went and broke the guy's leg.

Trainer: You broke his leg? That's pretty angry. What happened to make you that angry?

George: Well, it looked like a robbery to me, so it made me real angry and real jumpy.

Trainer: Was that on your job as a guard?

George: No, it didn't happen then.

Trainer: I see.

George: It looked like a robbery, and I tried to stop it. I broke his leg, so I wouldn't get stabbed or shot.

Trainer:	Okay. What about other examples? Examples in the home, or with other people. Cheryl, Ann? Not you, huh? Okay. Bob? Karen? What would be some examples of difficulty with self-control that might apply to you?
Karen:	Right now we have some friends staying with us. They've been with us for 2 weeks and they'll be staying with us 2 more weeks. They have four kids, and I have three of my own at home right now. It's really nerve wracking. I really have to grit my teeth. Sit and grit and it's hard.
Trainer:	The house has turned into a hotel, huh?
Karen:	Right.
Trainer:	That might be a good example, if you wouldn't mind, of something we could role play to get the group started in practicing using self-control. Karen, would you mind doing that?
Karen:	Okay.

ORGANIZING THE ROLE PLAY

Trainer:	Could you tell us a little more about it? What is the name of the person or the couple you might want to speak to if you wanted to say "It's time to go."
Karen:	Their names are Kim and Tom.
Trainer:	Kim and Tom, okay. Let's see, the first step is to tune in to what is going on in your body. How do you know when you're feeling angry? What do you actually feel?
Karen:	Well, my head starts hurting and I get pains in my stomach.
Trainer:	Mm-hmm. Okay. So the signals are pretty clear. You've already told us what happened to make you feel that way: they moved in and they unpacked and they're staying. With the four kids. Think about ways in which you might control yourself. This is a very important step because before you choose one way to control yourself you want to be sure you consider all alternatives. I mentioned five or six before. When you're feeling it in your head and in your stomach and you know why, what things might you consider to control yourself? What could you do?
Karen:	Most of the time I just try to ignore it.
Trainer:	Ignore it. That's a good way some of the time.
Karen:	Some of the time. It doesn't work all of the time.

Trainer:	And of course, if you're in a situation in which you can ignore it, that's great. If you're in a situation where the four kids and the two parents are sitting down at the dinner table saying "Karen, where's supper?", it's hard to ignore it. What else can you do besides ignore it?
Karen:	Usually, I tell Kim or Tom what the kids are doing and that I wish they wouldn't do it.
Trainer:	Whom might you tell, Kim or Tom?
Karen:	Most of the time, Kim.

Selecting the Co-Actor

Trainer:	Okay, let's role play that. Who in this group most reminds you of Kim? Maybe one of the parent aides in the group, for example. Could you pick one of the parent aides in the room who is most like Kim? (George whispers to Karen.) You're getting some help. That's good. Thanks, George. (Laughter) That is good because we want good casting. Who do you think, George, is most like Kim?
George:	Well, I don't know. Maybe the lady in the back.
Trainer:	Bernie? Or Joan?
George:	Joan.
Trainer:	What do you think, Karen? Should Joan do it? Are there things about Joan that are like Kim? We want to make this role play as realistic as possible.
Karen:	I think that Bea's more like Kim.
Trainer:	Bea, okay. Well, it's your role play, so let's pick Bea. Okay, George?
George:	(Throws up his hands)
Trainer:	We'll go with Bea. Is that okay with you?
Karen:	Okay.
Trainer:	Okay with you, Bea?
Bea:	Sure.
Trainer:	Tell us a little bit about Kim. When Bea gets up to role play, she's going to do the best job possible to act just like the real Kim would. What is Kim like?
Karen:	She's kind of snotty when it comes to the kids.
Trainer:	Snotty when it comes to the kids, okay.
Karen:	She gets offended when you tell her something.

Setting the Stage for Role Playing

Trainer: She's insulted easily. But, if you do it right, maybe that won't happen. That's what we're going to find out. Would you sit over here, Bea, and Karen, if you'd sit here so you can see Bea and the steps of the skill on the chalkboard at the same time. I'm going to be up here, pointing at the steps. Where might you talk to Kim? In your living room? In your kitchen?

Karen: Living room.

Trainer: Okay. We're in your living room now. You're sitting on what, the couch?

Karen: No, the rocker.

Trainer: On the rocker. Where is Kim sitting?

Karen: On the couch.

Trainer: You're on the couch, Kim. Is it quiet, or are the kids all around screaming?

Karen: They're all around screaming. (Laughter)

Final Instructions for Role Playing

Trainer: They're all around—well, let's keep it down, gang. Okay. Here's the scene. It's in the living room. Bea, you're Kim. Karen, you are yourself and you're starting to feel these things (pointing to the steps). I want you to say out loud what you'd really be thinking—what's going on inside you; what happened to make you feel that way; what different ways you might think about controlling yourself. Then choose a way and do it. If it involves talking to her for Step 4, then do it. If it involves ignoring her, walk away. Whatever you think is the best way for you to control yourself, do it. Okay? Bea, you say and do what you think Kim would do in reaction to what Karen says. Now, (to the group) you folks have an assignment while we're doing this. What I want you to do is watch the steps and see how well Karen does them. When we're through, we're going to give her feedback—tell her how well we think she did the steps. If there are any problems, we'll help her improve them. Okay? That's your assignment.

Okay, we're all ready now. We're going to start with Step 1. You tell us out loud, Karen, as you did a moment ago, what it is you're feeling in your body. Then we'll go to Step 2. Go ahead. Talk out loud, even though Kim is there.

ROLE PLAYING

Karen: Oh, I'm getting a headache and a tense feeling in my chest. I can't stand this. I'm going crazy. These kids are driving me nuts.

Trainer: Wait a moment, Kim. She's actually thinking out loud to herself. She's going to talk to you in a moment.

Karen: I told her a thousand times not to let the kids in the front room on my rug with drinks or food. They're getting it all on my new rug. I don't know. She just doesn't listen. I can't ignore it. I'll just sit here for a few minutes, take a few deep breaths, and then I'll try to talk to her about it. (Pause, takes three deep breaths) Kim, I really wish you wouldn't let the kids in the front room. I've asked you a lot of times. The rug is getting real dirty and I don't have the money for a cleaner. Will you try a little harder?

Kim: I could try, but I don't see how they're doing any harm. It's easy to pick up a spot on the rug. Does it bother you that much?

Karen: Well, maybe you should try cleaning it up sometimes.

Kim: I suppose I could do that.

Trainer: Okay, let's cut at that. I want you to go back to your seats now. (Applause)

PERFORMANCE FEEDBACK

Trainer: Is that the feedback then—we're saying she did a good job? Yes, did you feel she did a good job? Bea, if you were the actual Kim, what do you think you would do?

Kim: I couldn't yell at her for the way she handled the situation. I think she did a very nice job. I guess I would have just gone along with her, agreed, and told her I'd clean it up.

Trainer: Cheryl, could you tell us if Karen did Step 1 and, if she did, how?

Cheryl: Yes. I remember, because when I get angry the same thing happens. She said her head and chest hurt or felt tight.

Trainer: Good feedback. What about Step 2? Bob?

Bob: That's when she said about the kids and dirtying up the rug.

Trainer: That's excellent. So she was clear on deciding what upset her. For Step 3, did she think of different ways to control herself?

Harry: She thought about walking away or ignoring it.

Bob: She took deep breaths.

Trainer: What else did she do?

Ann: Well, she talked to Bea, I mean Kim. She told her to make her kids stop messing up.

Trainer: So she thought about alternatives, different ways to control herself—ignoring, deep breathing, talking to the other person. Then she chose the best two for her and did them. That was fine feedback and fine role playing. Now then, the key question is, Karen, could you actually do this—not with Bea, but with the real Kim?

Karen: Yeah, probably. I think I could.

HOMEWORK ASSIGNMENT

Trainer: Okay. Would you agree to have this be your homework assignment and tell us at the beginning of the next class how it worked?

Karen: Okay.

Trainer: Okay. Thanks very much.

Chapter Eight

Managing Problem Behaviors in the Structured Learning Group

As is true for any type of treatment, training, or teaching group, management problems sometimes occur during Structured Learning. Group management problems, at a general level, are any behaviors shown by one or more group members that interfere with, inhibit, deflect, or slow down the skills training procedures or goals that are the basic purposes of Structured Learning. In the present chapter we will describe problems as they may occur in the Structured Learning group. Some occur very rarely, others with somewhat greater frequency. All of the problems that we are presently aware of are included in our presentation to most fully prepare trainers for behaviors they may have to deal with in the actual groups. Our coverage should be considered comprehensive, but not exhaustive, since every time we have concluded that "we've seen everything" in the Structured Learning group, something new and challenging comes along. Our proposals for dealing with group management problems will usually suffice, but skilled trainers will be called upon from time to time to deal creatively and imaginatively with new challenges as they arise in even the most productive Structured Learning groups. Most methods for reducing group management problems will only need to be employed as a temporary bridge between initial trainee resistance or reluctance and that point in the process at which the trainee feels Structured Learning participation to be useful, valuable, and personally relevant. These techniques, derived from research on skills training group management as well as from our own experiences and those of others with such groups should enable trainers to deal with almost any difficulties that may arise in the Structured Learning group.

TYPES OF GROUP MANAGEMENT PROBLEMS

Table 2 lists the full range of group management problems that in reported experience have occurred in Structured Learning groups whose members are child abusive parents.

Inactivity

Minimal participation.   Minimal participation involves trainees who seldom volunteer, provide only brief answers, and in general give the trainers a feeling that they are "pulling teeth" to keep the group at its various skills training tasks.

Apathy.   A more extreme form of minimal participation is apathy, in which almost whatever the trainers do to direct, enliven, or activate the group, they are met with disinterest, lack of spontaneity, and little if any progress toward group goals.

Table 2. Types of Group Management Problems

I.   *Inactivity*
1. Minimal participation
2. Apathy
3. Falling asleep

II. *Active Resistance*
4. Participation, but not as instructed
5. Passive-aggressive isolation
6. Negativism
7. Disruptiveness

III. *Hyperactivity*
8. Digression
9. Monopolizing
10. Interruption
11. Excessive restlessness

IV. *Cognitive Inadequacies and Emotional Disturbance*
12. Inability to pay attention
13. Inability to understand
14. Inability to remember
15. Bizarre behavior

Falling asleep.   While it is quite rare, trainees do fall asleep from time to time. The sleepers need to be awakened and the trainers might wisely inquire into the cause of the tiredness, since boredom in the group, lack of sleep at home, and physical illness are all possible reasons, each one requiring a different trainer response.

Active Resistance

Participation, but not as instructed.   Trainees displaying this type of group management problem are "off target." They may be trying to role play, serve as co-actor, give accurate feedback, or engage in other tasks required in Structured Learning, but their own personal agendas or misperceptions interfere, and they wander off course to irrelevant or semi-irrelevant topics.

Passive-aggressive isolation.   Passive-aggressive isolation is not merely apathy, in which the trainees are simply disinterested in participating. Nor is it participation, but not as instructed, in which trainees actively go off task and raise personal agendas. Passive-aggressive isolation is the purposeful, intentional withholding of appropriate participation, an active shutting down of involvement. It can be thought of as a largely nonverbal crossing of one's arms in order to display deliberate nonparticipation.

Negativism.   When displaying negativism, trainees signal more overtly, by word and deed, the wish to avoid participation in the Structured Learning group. They may openly refuse to role play, provide feedback, or complete homework assignments. Or, they may not come to sessions, come late to sessions, or walk out in the middle of a session.

Disruptiveness.   Disruptiveness encompasses active resistance behaviors more extreme than negativism, such as openly and perhaps energetically ridiculing the trainers, other trainees, or aspects of the Structured Learning process. Or, disruptiveness may be shown by gestures, movements, noises, or other distracting nonverbal behaviors characteristically symbolizing overt criticism and hostility.

Hyperactivity

Digression.   Digression is related to participation, but not as instructed, but in our experience is a more repetitive, more determined, and more strongly motivated moving away from the purposes and procedures of Structured Learning. Here, the trainees are feeling strongly some emotion, such as anger or anxiety or despair, and are determined to express it. Or the skill portrayed by the trainers or other trainees may set off associations with important recent experiences, which the trainees feel the need to present and discuss. Digression is also often characterized by "jumping out of role" in the role play. Rather than merely wandering off track, in digression the trainees *drive* the train off its intended course.

Monopolizing. Monopolizing involves subtle and not so subtle efforts by trainees to get more than a fair share of time during a Structured Learning session. Long monologs, requests by the trainees to unnecessarily role play again, elaborate feedback, and attention-seeking efforts to "remain on stage" are examples of such monopolizing behavior.

Interruption. Similar to monopolizing, but more intrusive and insistent, interruption is literally breaking into the ongoing flow of a modeling display, role play, or feedback period with comments, questions, suggestions, observations, or other statements. Interruptions may be overly assertive, angry, or pungent on the one hand or take a more pseudobenevolent guise of being offered by a "trainer's helper." In either event, such interruptions more often than not retard the group's progress toward its goals.

Excessive restlessness. This is a more extreme, more physical form of hyperactivity. The trainees may fidget while sitting, rock their chairs, get up and pace, smoke a great deal, drink coffee after coffee, or display other nonverbal, verbal, gestural, or postural signs of restlessness. Such behavior will typically be accompanied by digression, monopolizing, or interrupting behavior.

Cognitive Inadequacies and Emotional Disturbance

Inability to pay attention. Closely related at times to excessive restlessness, the inability to pay attention is often an apparent result of internal or external distractions, daydreaming, or other pressing agendas that command the trainees' attention. Inability to pay attention except for brief time spans may also be due to one or more forms of cognitive impairment.

Inability to understand. Cognitive deficits due to developmental disability, intellectual inadequacy, impoverishment of experience, disease processes, or other sources may result in aspects of the Structured Learning process not being understood, or being misunderstood, by the trainees. Failure to understand can, of course, also result from errors in the clarity and complexity of statements presented by the trainers.

Inability to remember. Material presented in the Structured Learning group may be both attended to and understood by the trainees, but not remembered. This may result not only in problems of skill transfer, but also in group management problems when what is forgotten includes rules and procedures for trainee participation, homework assignments, and so forth.

Bizarre behavior.   This type of group management problem is not common in groups of abusive parents, but when instances of it do occur it can be especially disruptive to group functioning. It may not only pull other trainees off task, but it may also frighten them or make them highly anxious. The range of bizarre behaviors possible is quite broad, and includes talking to oneself or inanimate objects, offering incoherent statements to the group, becoming angry for no apparent reason, hearing and responding to imaginary voices, and exhibiting peculiar mannerisms.

REDUCING GROUP MANAGEMENT PROBLEMS

Most Structured Learning sessions proceed rather smoothly, but the competent trainer is a prepared trainer. Preparation includes both knowing what problems might occur, as well as corrective steps to take when they do occur. The remainder of this chapter will be devoted to examining an array of methods for reducing group management problems. The particular methods we and others have found to be especially useful are listed in Table 3.

Simplification Methods

Reward minimal trainee accomplishment.   Problematic trainee behavior can sometimes be altered by a process similar to what has been called "shaping." For example, rather than responding positively to trainees only when they enact a complete and accurate role play, reward in the form of praise and approval may be offered for lesser but still successful accomplishments. Perhaps only one or two behavioral steps were role played correctly. Or, in the extreme example of rewarding minimal trainee accomplishment, praise may be offered for "trying" after a totally unsuccessful role play, or even for merely paying attention to someone else's role play.

Shorten the role play.   A more direct means for simplifying the trainees' task is to ask less of them. One way of doing so is to shorten the role play, usually by asking trainees to role play only some (or one) of the behavioral steps that constitute the Structured Learning skill being taught.

Have trainer "feed" sentences to the trainee.   With trainees having a particularly difficult time participating appropriately in

Table 3. Methods for Reducing Group Management Problems

I. *Simplification Methods*
1. Reward minimal trainee accomplishment
2. Shorten the role play
3. Have trainer "feed" sentences to the trainee
4. Have trainee read a prepared script
5. Have trainee play co-actor role first

II. *Elicitation of Response Methods*
6. Call for volunteers
7. Introduce topics for discussion
8. Call on a specific trainee
9. Reinstruct trainees by means of prompting and coaching

III. *Threat Reduction Methods*
10. Employ additional live modeling by the trainers
11. Postpone trainee's role playing until last in sequence
12. Provide reassurance to the trainee
13. Provide empathic encouragement to the trainee
14. Clarify threatening aspects of the trainee's task
15. Restructure threatening aspects of the trainee's task

IV. *Termination of Response Methods*
16. Urge trainee to remain on task
17. Ignore trainee behavior
18. Interrupt ongoing trainee behavior

the Structured Learning group, especially for reasons of cognitive inadequacy, the trainer may elect to take on the role of coach or prompter. There are a variety of ways this may be accomplished, perhaps the most direct of which involves a trainer standing immediately behind the trainee and whispering the particular statements that constitute proper enactment of each behavioral step for the trainee to then say out loud.

Have trainee read a prepared script. We personally have never used this approach to group management problems, but others report some success with it. In essence, it removes the burden of figuring out what to say completely from the trainees and makes easier the task of getting up in front of the group and acting out the skill's behavioral steps. Clearly, as with all simplification methods, using a prepared script should be seen as a temporary device, used to move trainees in the direction of role playing with no such special assistance from the trainers.

Have trainee play co-actor role first.   An additional means of easing trainees into the responsibility of being the main actor in a role play is to have them play the role of the co-actor at first. This accustoms them more gradually to getting up before the group and speaking, because the "spotlight" is mostly on someone else. As with the use of a prepared script, this method should be used temporarily only. Before moving on to the next skill, *all* trainees must always take on the role of the main actor with the particular skill.

Elicitation of Response Methods

Call for volunteers.   Particularly in the early stages of the life of a Structured Learning group, trainee participation may have to be actively elicited by the group's trainers. As trainees actually experience the group's procedures, find them personally relevant and valuable, and find support and acceptance from the trainers and from other group members, the need for such elicitation typically diminishes. The least directive form of such trainer activity is the straightforward calling for volunteers.

Introduce topics for discussion.   Calling for volunteers, essentially an invitation to the group as a whole, may yield no response in the highly apathetic group. Under this circumstance, introducing topics for the group to discuss that appear relevant to the needs, concerns, aspirations, and particular skill deficiencies of the participants will often be an effective course of action to pursue.

Call on a specific trainee.   The largely nondirective elicitation methods already presented, if unsuccessful, may be followed by a more active and directive trainer intervention, namely calling upon a particular trainee and requesting that trainee's participation. It is often useful to select for such purposes a trainee who by means of attentiveness, facial expression, eye contact, or other nonverbal signaling communicates potential involvement and interest.

Reinstruct trainee by means of prompting and coaching.   The trainer may have to become still more active and directive than mentioned already and, in a manner similar to our earlier discussion of feeding role play lines to a trainee, prompt and coach the trainee to adequate participation. Such assistance may involve any aspect of the Structured Learning process—attending to the modeling display, following a skill's behavioral steps during role playing, providing useful performance feedback after someone else's role play, or completing homework assignments in the proper manner.

Threat Reduction Methods

Employ additional live modeling by the trainers.   When the Structured Learning trainers engage in live modeling of the session's skill, they are doing more than just the main task of skill enactment. Such trainer behavior also makes it easier for trainees to similarly get up and risk less-than-perfect performances in an effort to learn the skill. For trainees who are particularly anxious, inhibited, or reluctant to role play, an additional portrayal or two of the same skill by the trainers may put them at ease. Such additional live modeling will also prove useful to those trainees having difficulty role playing because of cognitive inadequacies.

Postpone   trainee's   role   playing   until   last   in sequence.   This recommendation is a straightforward extension of the one just presented. The threat of role playing may be reduced for trainees if they are not required to role play until both the trainers' live modeling and role playing by all other trainees are completed. It is crucial, though, that no trainee deficient in the session's skill be excused completely from role playing that skill. To do so would run counter to the central, skill-training purpose of Structured Learning.

Provide reassurance to the trainee.   This method of dealing with group management problems involves the trainers providing one or more trainees with brief, straightforward, simple, but very often highly effective, messages of encouragement and reassurance. "You can do it," "We'll help you as you go along," and "Take it a step at a time" are only a few examples of such frequently valuable reassurance.

Provide empathic encouragement to the trainee.   This is a method we have used often, with good results. In the case of trainee reluctance to role play, for example, the trainer may provide empathic encouragement by proceeding through the following steps:

Step 1.   Offer the resistant trainee the opportunity to explain in greater detail her reluctance to role play and listen nondefensively.

Step 2.   Clearly express your understanding of the resistant trainee's feelings.

Step 3. If appropriate, respond that the trainee's view is a viable alternative.

Step 4. Present your own view in greater detail, with both supporting reasons and probable outcomes.

Step 5. Express the appropriateness of delaying a resolution of the trainer-trainee difference.

Step 6. Urge the trainee to tentatively try to role play the given behavioral steps.

The identical procedure may be used effectively with a wide range of other trainee resistances.

Clarify threatening aspects of the trainee's task. Clarifying threatening aspects of tasks requires deeper explanations, repetition of earlier clarifications, and provision of further illustrations. In all instances, the task involved remains unchanged, but what is required of trainees to complete the task is further presented and made clear.

Restructure threatening aspects of the trainee's task. Unlike the method just discussed, in which the task remains unchanged and the trainers seek to clarify the trainee's understanding of it, in the present method the trainers may alter the trainee's task if it is seen as threatening. Behavioral steps may be altered, simplified, moved around, deleted, or added. Role plays may be shortened, lengthened, changed in content, merged with other skills, or otherwise changed. Aspects of performance feedback may be changed, too—the sequence of who delivers it, its generality versus specificity, its timing, its length, its focus. *No* aspect of Structured Learning as presented in this book should be considered unchangeable. *All* treatment, training, and teaching methods should perpetually be open to revision as needed in the judgment of their skilled and sensitive users. Most certainly, this also includes Structured Learning.

Termination of Response Methods

Urge trainee to remain on task. Gently, but firmly, trainees who wander off the group's task may at times be brought back on track. The trainers can do this by reminders, cajoling, admonishing, or simply pointing out to them clearly what they are doing incorrectly and what they ought to be doing instead.

Ignore trainee behavior. Certain inappropriate trainee behaviors can be terminated most effectively by simply ignoring them. This withdrawal of reinforcement, or extinction process, is best applied to those problem behaviors that the group can tolerate while still remaining on task as the extinction process is taking place. Behaviors such as pacing, whispering to oneself, and occasional interruptions are examples of behaviors perhaps best terminated by simply ignoring them. Behaviors that are more disruptive, or even dangerous, will have to be dealt with more frontally.

Interrupt ongoing trainee behavior. This problem management method requires directive and assertive trainer behavior. We recommend interrupting ongoing trainee behavior primarily when other methods fail. Interrupting trainees' inappropriate, erroneous, or disruptive behavior should be carried out firmly, unequivocally, and with the clear message that the group has its tasks and they must be gotten on with. In its extreme form, interrupting trainee behavior may even require removing trainees from groups for a brief or extended period of time.

Chapter Nine

Structured Learning in the Agency Context

This chapter is designed for agency administrators and supervisors who are interested in implementing Structured Learning training. It describes Alliance, a coordination agency for those working with child abuse in Syracuse, New York, that has used Structured Learning with abusive parents since 1977. Our goal in this chapter is to provide a useful example of an agency and service environment where Structured Learning has been used with success. It further describes why Alliance first became interested in Structured Learning and the associated funding and implementation problems that occurred. We also seek in this chapter to provide a contextual sense of why, in this agency's experience, Structured Learning has proven to be a highly effective therapeutic intervention for abusive parents.

DESCRIPTION OF ALLIANCE

Alliance is a child and elder abuse coordination program that began in 1972 as a result of the tragic beating death of a 4-year-old child in Onondaga County, located in central New York State. The death probably could have been avoided had members of the investigation, education, and treatment community been working closely together, and if a regular vehicle for communication and an effective means for relating their findings to the court had been in place.

In response to this death and related events, a community task force visited Denver, Colorado, and the Kempe-Helfer program for coordinating agencies concerned with child abuse and became convinced that Onondaga County needed a shared agency philosophy and methods of coordination in the investigation and treatment of child abuse. The groundwork was established and agency coordination was developed to create Alliance. Alliance still depends strongly on the advisory board that created the organization, which has the Commissioners of Health, Mental Health, and Social Services or their designates as members, as well as a number of citizens and relevant practitioners. The board, called the Child Abuse Council, is appointed by the county executive. Many of the "turf" issues that are common in communities are able to be resolved because of the county executive's and the council's involvement in the process. Alliance and the Child Abuse Council interact with several levels of personnel within agencies to establish and maintain effective coordination: top administrators, middle management, and direct service workers.

Alliance currently serves over 700 families who are involved in, or are likely to become involved in, episodes of child abuse. Referrals are accepted from the Department of Social Services on all cases of physical and sexual abuse of children, failure to thrive in infancy due to parental deprivation, and prenatal prevention of potential abuse. Alliance has the responsibility for coordination of services for these families from investigation through treatment and is usually involved in cases for 1 or more years. As Figure 2 depicts, Alliance utilizes the services of all the health, mental health, social services, education, and law enforcement agencies in the community. As a case is referred, a treatment team is developed based on the needs of a particular family. An Alliance coordinator then convenes the multidisciplinary team, which includes the parents, approximately once a month to identify problems, establish and refine treatment plans, and clarify roles of the treatment providers. Each team meeting ends with team members, including the parents, taking responsibility for a particular aspect of the treatment plan. Treatment plans are concrete and behaviorally oriented, and each plan is evaluated at the beginning of the next team meeting.

None of the human services providers are paid for attendance at Alliance meetings; it is assumed that their participation is part of their role in doing effective intervention. Alliance staff also provides direct service to families through paid parent aides. These are individuals hired by Alliance because of their common sense, their life experiences, and their striking qualities of nurturing, caring, and believing in clients' ability to change. Their educational backgrounds vary from not completing high school to completing a master's degree. They give advice; act as role models; help break down the isolation of the parents by going with them to community services; assist in the clients' homes with household management, nutrition, parenting, and in other ways; and are available to clients 24 hours a day in time of crisis. Parent aides spend 4 to 8 hours a week with each family.

Figure 2. Typical Alliance Community Team*

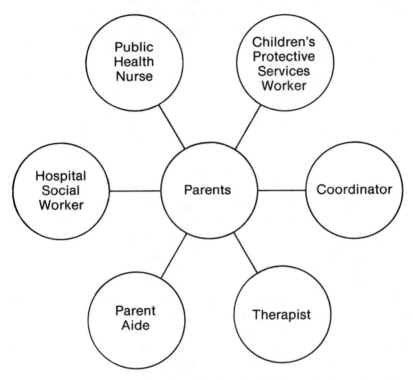

*Team composition varies depending on needs of family and/or services provided.

Alliance has a budget of almost a million dollars a year. It is funded by the Onondaga County Department of Social Services, the United Way, Catholic Charities (of which Alliance is a Division), and a multiplicity of other grants and funding sources.

ALLIANCE AND STRUCTURED LEARNING

In the mid 1970s, Alliance's coordination program was fully implemented in the community, and there were a number of therapeutic agencies and private practitioners who participated on Alliance teams and saw abusive parents and their children in individual family sessions or groups. Alliance had overcome some of its early confidentiality hurdles in getting therapists to be part of its teams and to work with Children's Protective Services and the courts. Availability of therapeutic resources was not a major problem; getting the client population to attend therapy sessions on a regular basis *was* a problem. Parents gave many reasons for failure to attend or to follow through, such as "transportation problems" or "I forgot," but most often and most importantly they said, "It doesn't do any good, and I don't know why I should go."

Coordinators at Alliance were caught in a dilemma. They knew their client population was in desperate need of therapeutic services, but the services that were available were not being used effectively by most clients. Clients thought in concrete and behavioral terms; therapists thought more abstractly and psychodynamically. Clients had poor ego strength and development, were poor planners, and could not make decisions or decide what was most important in a given situation. Traditional therapies required that clients look inward and draw on their past experiences to understand and solve current problems. For adults who had suffered extreme emotional and physical deprivation throughout their childhoods and who had grown up in environments where violence and not discussion was the response to a problem, or who had grown up isolated with few or no friends and who lacked even the most minimal social skills, the inward and backward look was painful and very typically not productive. Rather than drawing strength from their backgrounds and experience, they drew pain, confusion, and failure. It is little wonder that they found the openness and nondirectiveness of therapeutic sessions anxiety producing, confusing, and very often useless. In short, therapists had a vast array of skills to help the insight-oriented client who could describe feelings and utilize her past to help deal with the present. Conversely, the clients at Alliance had a vast array of therapeutic needs, but the traditional approaches and tools did not match their resources.

While traditional therapy was not working with most of Alliance's parents, teams involving parent aides, public health nursing, neighborhood outreach programs, and Children's Protective Services did work. Parent aides were a significant key to these successful treatment teams as they began to reparent abusive parents to overcome the horrendous early nurturing deficits that are such striking aspects of abusive parents' backgrounds. They gave warmth, nurturance, and love to the damaged and emotionally scarred adults who then began to build their own resource pool so that they could in turn give love to their children. Alliance staff members began to wonder if it would be possible to teach parents some basic skills, not only by informal example and instruction, but also in a more systematic and structured manner, while still providing the personal, intense, individual relationship that parent aides were offering.

In the mid-1970s, discussion began about using Structured Learning with abusive parents. Structured Learning's concreteness, common sense, and simplicity—as well as its demonstrated success with other types of clients—sounded right for Alliance's population. But how could the Alliance staff get group-shy, skill deficient, no-show clients to attend Structured Learning even if it would work? With graduate student assistance and donations of bus tokens, baby-sitting services, and donuts, Alliance began its first Structured Learning group. Parent aides were taught to be trainers, and other groups began. Attendance was near perfect, parental enthusiasm was extraordinary, and parent aides began reporting that clients were often using the skills they learned in Structured Learning in their home settings. Many parents who also needed traditional therapeutic services but previously could not utilize them seemed to be able to do so in combination with Structured Learning. They reported feeling better about themselves and they seemed better able to express their feelings. Their self-control, parenting, communication, and decision-making skills were anecdotally documented as improved by other professionals on Alliance teams and, perhaps most significantly, by the clients themselves.

Most of Alliance's client population is on welfare; many are second and third generation welfare families. Many of Alliance's clients have some degree of retardation, developmental disability, mental illness, or have been labeled "character disordered." What the client population shares, whether on welfare or from the middle or upper income groups, is skill deficiency; yet somehow almost all seemed able to function effectively in the Structured Learning groups. Thus, the staff was free from the painful screening process that in the past had frequently ruled out the participation of abusive parents in many other types of groups.

Parent aide group leaders worked long and hard in developing live modeling displays that used both examples with which parents could identify and language that the parents could understand. The only group of clients who presented difficulty for Structured Learning group leaders were those whose degree of mental retardation was so pronounced that they slowed down the rest of the group. For those clients, parent aides sought to provide more slowly paced groups.

The most common client complaint about the Structured Learning group was "Why were there only eight sessions, and couldn't it continue?" Diplomas were given to the parents at the completion of their "Structured Learning course." These diplomas were often prominently displayed in homes that were so disorganized that one could hardly find a chair.

Why did Structured Learning seem to work so well with the parents at Alliance while other treatments failed? Did parents come to the groups because transportation, donuts, and child care were provided? Did they come because their parent aides, their trusted friends and advisors, asked them to come and went with them? Did they come because of the warmth and support of the parent aide group leaders or the warmth and support of the other group members? Did they come because of the modeling displays and structure of the group? Or did they come because their skill learning was paying off where it counted, at home? Our conclusion is that all of these factors were important contributors to why Structured Learning worked.

FUNDING EFFORTS FOR STRUCTURED LEARNING

Throughout the 1970s, Goldstein and Erné explored a multitude of funding sources so that Structured Learning could be made available for more clients and in order to teach a wider range of skills. Despite its apparent success and relative inexpensiveness, funding for Structured Learning proved difficult to obtain. The reasons given were "It can't be funded by Mental Health, though it sounds like a great approach; it should be funded by the Department of Social Services" or "It can't be funded by the Department of Social Services, though it sounds like a great approach; it should be funded by Mental Health." Structured Learning did not fit into any one system of service delivery, and regardless of its effectiveness in human and financial terms, it could not be fully institutionalized. Goldstein, Erné, the Alliance staff, the parents, and the community believed in Structured Learning, but that belief was not being translated into program dollars. The parent aides, in frustration, began making and selling crafts on their own time to help pay for Structured Learning. Despite their countless hours of voluntary time and commitment, there was not enough money to offer Structured Learning to many of Alliance's clients.

Finally in 1982, the New York State Office of Mental Retardation and Developmental Disability (OMRDD) responded favorably to a grant application for Alliance to do Structured Learning for 1 year with 45 clients who were mentally ill, mentally retarded, or both. In 1983, OMRDD funded a second year of the grant to evaluate Structured Learning (discussed in Chapter Ten). In 1984, Alliance was funded by its primary funding source, the Onondaga County Department of Social Services, to include Structured Learning as part of the Parent Aide Service, and Structured Learning was further expanded to do a combined Head Start-Alliance accelerated program for children and parents where both parent aides and Structured Learning were utilized. The OMRDD grant provided funds to develop videotapes for modeling displays instead of relying on live modeling by the group's leaders. The parents, frequent watchers of television, readily accepted the videotape displays and the quality and effectiveness of Structured Learning was further improved.

It is our expectation and hope as we look to the future that the use and impact of Structured Learning with abusive parents—at Alliance and elsewhere—will continue to grow, thus adding in significant ways to the lives of such clients, as well as the children for whom they are responsible.

Chapter Ten

Structured Learning Research

Since 1970, our research group has conducted a systematic research program oriented toward evaluating and improving the effectiveness of Structured Learning. Approximately 50 investigations have been conducted involving a wide variety of trainee populations.* These include chronic adult schizophrenics (Goldstein, 1973; Goldstein et al., 1976; Liberman, 1970; Orenstein, 1973; Sutton-Simon, 1973), geriatric patients (Lopez, 1977; Lopez, Hoyer, Goldstein, Gershaw, & Sprafkin, 1980), young children (Hummel, 1979; Swanstrom, 1974), such change-agent trainees as mental hospital staff (Berlin, 1974; Goldstein & Goodhart, 1973; Lack, 1975; Robinson, 1973; Schneiman, 1972), policemen (Goldstein, Monti, Sardino, & Green, 1977), persons employed in industrial contexts (Goldstein & Sorcher, 1973, 1974), and in recent years aggressive and other behaviorally disordered adolescents (Goldstein et al., 1980; Greenleaf, 1978; Litwack, 1976; Trief, 1977; Wood, 1977) and, as this chapter will detail, child abusing parents (Fischman, 1984, 1985; Heiko, 1980; Solomon, 1977).

At a broad level of generalization, these several empirical evaluations of Structured Learning combine to yield two central conclusions:

1. Skill acquisition. (Do trainees *learn* the skills?)

Across diverse trainee populations and target skills, skill acquisition is a reliable training outcome, occurring in well over 90 percent of Structured Learning trainees. While pleased with this outcome, we are acutely aware of the manner in which therapeutic gains demonstrable in the training context are rather easily accomplished—given the potency, support, encouragement, and lack of

---

*These investigations are reported and examined in the citations noted as well as the books *Structured Learning Therapy* (Goldstein, 1973), *Skill Training for Community Living* (Goldstein et al., 1976), *Skillstreaming the Adolescent* (Goldstein et al., 1980), *Skillstreaming the Elementary School Child* (McGinnis & Goldstein, 1984), and, especially, *Psychological Skill Training* (Goldstein, 1981).

threat of trainers and therapists in that context. The more conse-quential outcome question by far pertains to trainee skill perform-ance in real-world contexts (i.e., skill transfer).

2. Skill transfer. (Do trainees *use* the skills in real-life settings?)

Across diverse trainee populations, target skills, and applied (real-world) settings, skill transfer occurs with approximately 50 percent of Structured Learning trainees. Goldstein and Kanfer (1979) as well as Karoly and Steffen (1980) have indicated that across several dozen types of psychotherapy involving many different types of psy-chopathology, the average transfer rate on followup is between 15 percent and 20 percent of patients seen. The 50 percent rate conse quent to Structured Learning is a significant improvement upon this collective base rate, though it must immediately be underscored that this cumulative average transfer finding also means that the gains shown by half of our trainees were limited to in-session acquisition. Of special consequence, however, is the consistently clear manner in which skill transfer in our studies was a function of the explicit imple-mentation of laboratory derived transfer-enhancing techniques.

In the present chapter, we wish to focus in particular upon the four Structured Learning evaluation studies whose trainee samples were abusive parents. Their combined outcomes clearly confirm that the two broad conclusions drawn—very high levels of skill acquisi-tion, more modest but enhancer-associated levels of skill transfer—also apply to these Structured Learning trainees.

Study 1. Mastery Induction and Helper Structuring as Transfer Enhancers in Teaching Self-control to Abusive Parents (Solomon, 1977)

A major direction taken by the behavior modification movement in recent years as part of its dual focus upon cognitive variables and self-instructional techniques has been procedures aimed at helping the individual develop a sense of control and even mastery over dif-ficult or threatening circumstances that he may be facing. Bandura's (1973) notion of self-efficacy, Frank's (1978) views on avoidance of demoralization, and Kazdin and Wilcoxon's (1976) perspective on the importance of the individual's expectancy for change are examples of this stance.

A number of persons have sought to relate this perspective to transfer enhancement. If, they hold, the individual not only sees his overt coping behavior working but, in addition, he attributes the success to his own efforts and skills, he is much better able in subsequent problem confrontations to have the motivation and self-confidence to be successful again. Consistent with this view is Lang's (1968) proposal that failure to transfer is a direct result of failure to alter cognitive sets when changing an individual's overt behavior. In response to this view, D'Zurilla and Goldfried (1971) sought to counteract failures of transfer by a technique they termed cognitive restructuring. Here, past situations that have been explained in person-as-victim terms are relabeled with more rational explanations, often involving mastery. In the subsequent problem situation, the individual is encouraged to make appropriate control and mastery ("can do") self-statements that serve to cue adaptive behavioral responses.

This effect of a sense of control and mastery on the transfer of positive behaviors is not without experimental support. Goldfried and Trier (1974) found that representing relaxation training to clients as a self-control procedure increased maintenance of therapeutic gains more effectively than did portraying relaxation as an automatic anxiety-reducing technique. Liberman (1970), whose procedures for mastery manipulation were used in the study by Solomon that we will be examining, falsely informed a sample of psychotherapy outpatients that their success on a series of tasks was due to their own efforts. These patients maintained their therapeutic improvement on a 3-month followup, while those not subjected to this mastery manipulation did not. Valins and Ray (1967) have reported analogous results in other experimental contexts.

The study by Solomon (1977) that we will look at examined the transfer-enhancing potency of this self-attribution process in the context of skill training for self-control in an abusive parent sample. In a beginning effort to discern the joint impact of combinations of potential transfer-enhancing techniques, the mastery manipulation experimental conditions were crossed with a second factor, helper structuring (the belief that one will have to teach to others the Structured Learning skill one is now learning), which proved promising for transfer-enhancing purposes in Litwack's (1976) investigation of Structured Learning and transfer with adolescents.

Study procedures were operationalized in a 2 × 2 plus Brief Instructions control group factorial design as schematically depicted in Figure 3. Participants in this investigation were 40 abusive parents affiliated with a child abuse service agency in a large metropolitan area. Of the 31 women and 9 men in the study (assigned randomly, not proportionately, to study conditions), 38 were white and 2 were

Figure 3. Experimental Design for Solomon (1977) Mastery Induction—Helper Structuring Study

Helper Structuring

		Present	Absent
Mastery Induction	Present	I	II
	Absent	III	IV

V
(Brief Instr.
Control)

Reprinted from *Psychological skill training: The structured learning technique* by Arnold P. Goldstein, 1981, Pergamon Press.

black. Nineteen were married and 21 were single. Study participation, as in all of our investigations, was on a volunteer basis following a description to all potential trainees of study procedures and goals.

The study's target skill, self-control, was operationalized by the following behavioral steps:

1. Think about what is happening to make you feel that you are about to lose control.
2. Think about what you could do that would help you control yourself.
3. Consider what might happen if you did each of these things.
4. Choose the best way to control yourself and do it.

Study assessment procedures, as in most of our Structured Learning investigations, were focused on the learning of overt behaviors (the skill's behavioral steps). Trainees were exposed to an extended series of created stimulus situations in which the study skill would be an appropriate response and rated for the correspondence of their actual response to the skill's behavioral steps. Both stimulus situations identical to those employed during the Structured Learning sessions (the Direct Test), and novel, never-seen-before situations (the Minimal and Extended Generalization Tests) were used—thus providing, respectively, behavioral measures of both skill acquisition and skill transfer. The specific stimulus situations employed in the Direct Test included:

1. You're sitting in the living room watching your favorite soap opera. It's been a long day and you're really tired. Your child starts whining and says, "I'm hungry, get me something to eat. I want something to eat now!"

2. It's breakfast time and you've just put a bowl of cereal on the table for your child. You turn around to pour yourself a cup of coffee and turn back when you hear a crash to see the bowl broken into pieces with milk and cereal all over the floor.

3. It's about time for you to leave for school. You are all ready to go when you hear the news report that the day care center where your kids go will be closed because of a water main break. You are really angry about this and say, "Go to your room and play." But the kids won't listen and start fighting.

4. It's noon and your child has just come back from the day care center. You're fixing his lunch when he says, "I don't want that shit for lunch. Give me something else."

Each study participant, as a part of agency procedures for all of its clients, was assigned to a parent aide who functioned in the participant's home in a variety of helping capacities. Generalization test information for this investigation was obtained from these parent aides who were trained to make reliable observations of the presence and absence of self-control behaviors in response to real-life, in-the-home stimuli that chronically instigate loss of self-control.

Participants assigned to study Conditions I-IV participated in two 2-hour Structured Learning sessions targeted to self-control. Prior to training, participants assigned to the two Mastery Induction cells (I and II) underwent a procedure designed after that developed by Liberman (1970). Essentially, it was a reaction time task in which they had to discriminate between lights of different colors. In describing the task, the experimenter led the parents to believe that it was directly related to self-control and that success with this task would lead to, or be indicative of, improvement in ability to maintain self-control in difficult situations. The instructions were as follows:

In this task you will learn to improve your control over your feelings and actions. You will know when you are starting to get angry and will be able to stop yourself from acting on it and getting in trouble. As you improve in this skill you will be able to be more in control and make good choices about what to do when you get tense. This way you can find other ways to blow off steam that won't hurt you or anyone else. This skill plus your own control over yourself will help you improve relationships with others. You may find it easier to get along better with members of your family and may feel better about yourself. As you gain more control over yourself you may have better control over the way you are with others and improve the way you get along with them.

Then the experimenter explained the reaction time task in the following way:

In front of you there is a panel with four different colored lights and four buttons. One button is in front of each light. What I would like you to do is to rest your hand in front of the panel. When the light comes on I want you to push the button that matches the light as fast as possible. Try to push the button as soon as you can after the light comes on. You will be given a few practice trials and then I will begin to record whether you pushed the correct button and how fast you are. Remember to try to go as fast as you can. Get ready and we will take a few practice trials.

Each parent was given three practice trials and asked if there were any questions. Then the parent was given 10 recorded trials. At the end of this session, the experimenter gave the parent feedback on her performance. The feedback, however, was unrelated to actual performance. Instead, it was structured to indicate progressive improvement over the course of the trials. The reaction time task was given once more during training but prior to any posttesting. For the first reaction time session the parent was told that on 4 trials her reaction time was faster than average but that on 6 trials it was too slow. For the second reaction time session the parent was told that her reaction times were faster than that of the average population on all of the trials. The experimenter attributed the "improved" performance to something the person must have been doing, that is, her own efforts at doing it more quickly, and that it was expected that she would maintain this improvement. The experimenter added that this control would be useful to the parent for controlling feelings and actions in general.

Helper Structuring Induction (cells I and III) directly paralleled Litwack's (1976) instructions:

There are others who would like help in learning how to better control themselves in difficult situations. We think you could be helpful to them by teaching them the skills that you learn. Being a member of this group will prepare you to be able to be good helpers. (p. 39)

During the subsequent Structured Learning training itself, the expectation of later serving as a helper was reiterated, that is, prior to tape listening, the trainer would say, "Remember to listen carefully to the tape because you will be teaching this to another person" or after successful role playing, "That was really good. Learning the steps so well will help you teach it to others."

Means and standard deviations for each experimental condition on all study measures are presented in Table 4.

As these data make clear, participation in Structured Learning (I-IV) led to significantly higher levels of skill acquisition than did a No Training (Brief Instructions) control experience. Self-control skill acquisition was a clear study outcome. This study's other between-condition differences bear upon the issue of transfer enhancement. Analyses of variance across conditions (2×2) are given in Table 5.

These analyses of variance reveal a significant overall effect for mastery induction on the acquisition and transfer of self-control on

Table 4. Means and Standard Deviations for Solomon (1977) Study Conditions

CONDITION	DIRECT TEST (PRE)	DIRECT TEST (POST)	MINIMAL GEN'L	EXTENDED GEN'L
I Mastery plus Helper				
X	5.18	25.13	21.13	16.63
SD	1.77	7.40	6.13	5.66
II Mastery				
X	8.25	19.63	17.50	15.38
SD	2.49	6.50	5.63	5.40
III Helper				
X	5.13	13.75	14.38	9.13
SD	2.75	2.44	2.39	5.03
IV No Mastery-No Helper				
X	6.50	13.50	13.00	6.50
SD	2.20	3.02	2.50	2.78
V Brief Instructions				
X	4.88	5.25	4.25	3.00
SD	3.23	3.88	3.37	0.00

Reprinted with permission from *Psychological skill training: The structured learning technique* by Arnold P. Goldstein, 1981, Pergamon Press.

Table 5. Analysis of Variance (F) for Solomon (1977) Study Conditions

SOURCE	DIRECT TEST (POST)	MINIMAL GEN'L	EXTENDED GEN'L
Mastery	19.69*	12.46*	25.95*
Helper	.12	2.46	1.45
Mastery × Helper	.73	.50	.18

*p < .01

Reprinted with permission from *Psychological skill training: The structured learning technique* by Arnold P. Goldstein, 1981, Pergamon Press.

all three study dependent measures. Post hoc Newman-Keuls cell comparisons across these data reveal that parents receiving both mastery induction and helper structuring (cell I) show levels of self-control significantly greater than all other study conditions for acquisition and minimal generalization. On extended generalization, both mastery induction plus helper structuring, and mastery induction alone, led to significantly greater target skill level than the other study conditions. As shown in Table 4 helper-structuring effects were consistently in the direction predicted, but were not statistically significant.

It seems appropriate, given these findings, to conclude our consideration of this investigation by quoting Solomon's (1977) summary observation:

> The present study offers further support for the clinical utility of attribution theory. The results suggest that when a patient views himself as responsible for his improvement in therapy he is more likely to maintain the gains made. . . . Parents in this study receiving the Mastery manipulation developed an increased sense of mastery over one part of their environment and in doing so may have developed more positive expectations regarding competent performance in areas where they had previously met with little success. Their belief that they were responsible for changes in their behavior on the reaction time task may have fostered the belief that their success at self-control in the groups was due to their own efforts. Thus, they were more likely to apply this skill to new situations than parents who did not receive the mastery component. The implication for therapy with abusive parents is that the inculcation of the expectation of the efficacy of one's own

efforts in changing the abusive pattern may be the essential element in generalizing therapeutic gains. (pp. 49–50)

Study 2. Consultee-Centered and Problem-Solving Consultation Services to Paraprofessionals Working with Child Abusing Parents in a Structured Learning Therapy Program (Heiko, 1980)

Heiko's (1980) investigation will be examined much more briefly than the others presented in this chapter, since its main focus, comparing different consultation interventions, is not relevant to our present theme. As an important side-focus of her study, however, skill acquisition consequences of Structured Learning were examined and should be reported here.

Working out of a consultation theory perspective, Heiko was not able to demonstrate outcome differences as a result of differing consultation styles and substance provided to parent aides before and during the Structured Learning sessions conducted by these aides. However, of direct relevance to our concern here, across all three consultation conditions abusive parents showed significant pre- to postprogram gain in the study skill, self-control, as a result of Structured Learning. Furthermore, from the parents' perspective, self-control skill transfer also appears to have occurred. Heiko comments:

> Parents indicated that they felt they 'got along' better with others in general after having participated in the program ($p < .005$).* In addition, they indicated that they felt more positively about their partners ($p < .064$) and family members ($p < .018$) since the SLT program had commenced. For all groups there was a significant indication that parents thought they had learned self-control skills after attending the SLT program ($p < .011$). Parent responses to a followup question . . . showed significantly positive responses to the question of whether the SLT program helped that parent to control her or himself ($p < .004$). (p. 30)

Study 3. Evaluating the Effectiveness of Structured Learning with Abusive Parents (Fischman, 1984)

Our third investigation of the effectiveness of Structured Learning with abusive parents was intentionally designed to be a more difficult skill acquisition test in three ways. First, its participating trainees were 54 parents who, in addition to their histories of abusive

---

*Based on Wilcoxin test analyses of relevant questionnaire data.

behavior toward their children, were also developmentally disabled. Second, Structured Learning's effectiveness was tested against both attention control and no-treatment control conditions. Finally, effectiveness was examined by means of a "staggered start" design across three target skills (Using Self-control, Setting Problem Priorities, Expressing Affection), thus permitting a series of effectiveness comparisons. The study's experimental design is depicted schematically in Figure 4.

The 54 participating abusive parents were randomly assigned to six groups of nine members each. Groups 1 and 2 began their Structured Learning participation immediately, with the three study target skills being taught during the first 3-week period (period A), and the subsequent 6 weeks (periods B and C) being spent in learning additional Structured Learning skills *not* a part of study measurement. Groups 3 and 4 spent the first 3 weeks of the study as a no-treatment control group (period D) and then, as had been done earlier for groups 1 and 2, went on in the second 3-week period (period E) to be taught the three study target skills. Period F involved the teaching of nontargeted skills. Groups 5 and 6 constituted the investigation's attention control condition, in which for 6 weeks (periods G and H, group members discussed various parenting, personal, and interpersonal concerns, but participated not at all in modeling, role playing, feedback, or other Structured Learning procedures relevant to the three target skills. Such training did occur following this attention control experience (in period I).

The staggered start, multiple-controls approach in this investigation was designed and implemented to permit several comparisons to be made that test the effectiveness of Structured Learning. Note that the comparisons of interest, that is, those testing the presence versus absence of Structured Learning on skill acquisition or transfer, are A versus D, A versus G, E versus D, and I versus H.

Three measures were used in this experiment. The Direct Test consisted of videotaped vignettes, four for each study skill, depicting real-life situations in response to which the given skill would be an appropriate and effective reaction. The Direct Test was administered both as a pretest and after each 3-week period of study participation, and the same stimulus situations were used as training stimuli during Structured Learning. It functioned, therefore, as the measure of skill acquisition. The Minimal Generalization Test similarly consisted of four relevant stimulus situations per study skill, but these were not displayed to the parent before or during study participation, only afterwards. In this manner, its use sought to discern whether parents

Figure 4. Staggered Start Experimental Design of Fischman (1984) Investigation

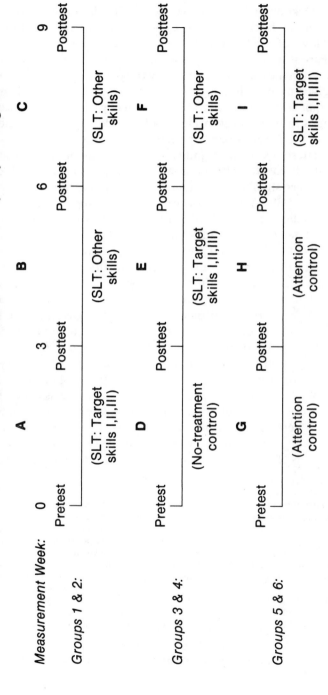

could make skilled responses to new skill-relevant situations to which they had not been previously exposed—in either pretesting or training. Moving from taped stimulus situations to a more real-life context, the Parent Aide Rating Scale formed the third, more extended generalization measure. Completed by the parent aide who functioned in the given parent's home, this measure provided at 3-week intervals a rating of at-home use of the study skills by the parent, as well as any changes in major presenting problems identified by the aide at the start of the parent's participation in this study.

There were no significant acquisition, minimal transfer, or extended transfer effects shown for the skill Using Self-control.* There were significant acquisition and minimal transfer effects in the Fischman (1984) study, however, for Expressing Affection and for Setting Problem Priorities. For Expressing Affection, Direct Test results ($F = 11.38, p < .01$) and Minimal Generalization Test results ($F = 3.47, p < .05$) permitted post hoc between-condition Tukey test analyses that revealed that for both skill acquisition and minimal transfer, parents receiving Structured Learning obtained significantly greater skill competence scores (number of the skills' behavioral steps) than did either no-treatment or attention control parents. The identical result emerged for Setting Problem Priorities. Significant analysis of variance results for the Direct Test ($F = 4.43, p < .05$) and Minimal Generalization Test ($F = 3.88, p < .05$) led to post hoc Tukey test cell comparisons revealing significant superiority on skill competence for Structured Learning trained parents versus those assigned to either control condition and, as with Expressing Affection, no significant difference between the control conditions. Thus, on two of the three study skills, this study—as was true for the two studies reported earlier in this chapter—finds a significant effect for Structured Learning

---

*We have obtained results parallel to these in our Structured Learning research with chronically aggressive juvenile delinquents, that is, other skills are acquired and transferred, but self-control appears not to be. We speculated in that context that the problem was largely one of a particularly short fuse. That is, people for whom an aggressive act is a prepotent, near-at-hand response to provocation will typically act out in response to provocation even when prosocial alternative skills are also in—but lower in—their response hierarchies. Our reaction to this speculation has been to augment Structured Learning skill training with another regular training sequence, Anger Control Training, a series of techniques explicitly designed to "lengthen the fuse." Based upon the work of Novaco (1975) and Feindler, Marriott, and Iwata (1984), our effort here to combine augmenting the prosocial with diminishing the antisocial has borne initial success with aggressive, delinquent youngsters (Goldstein, Glick, Zimmerman, Reiner, Coultry, & Gold, in press). Whether such a combined intervention would similarly result in increased self-control for abusive parents is clearly a research question deserving careful examination.

on skill acquisition, as well as for minimal transfer. In no instances, however, were there between-condition differences in the home, as reflected in the analysis of the Parent Aide Rating Scales. This last finding is crucial. It is valuable to know that abusive parents can be successfully taught prosocial skills, and that they can demonstrate such skills in response to novel, skill-relevant situations during testing at the agency, but the bottom line in this training effort occurs at home. The failure of skill performance to generalize to the home setting in this investigation is a major concern and led directly to the final investigation we wish to report, one in which a spectrum of potential transfer-enhancing procedures were added to the basic Structured Learning intervention in an energetic effort to obtain this vital last step—transfer to the home environment.

Study 4. The Use of Transfer Enhancers in Teaching Self-control and Empathy to Abusive Parents (Fischman, 1985)

Having demonstrated quite substantially—via the three investigations presented thus far—both the skill *acquisition* and *minimal generalization* potency of Structured Learning with abusive parents, we turn more fully in our next study to the topic of *extended* skill transfer. Forty-seven abusive parents participated in this investigation. Its target Structured Learning skills were Using Self-control and Empathy. Three experimental conditions were constituted and compared in a 1 × 3 experimental format, as shown in Figure 5.

Conditions II and III paralleled directly their implementation in Fischman's (1984) investigation, that is, periods A and G respectively. Condition I, however, added a full array of potentially transfer-enhancing techniques to the basic Structured Learning intervention. These included:

1. *Overlearning.* In contrast to parents assigned to Condition II, in which each trainee modeled and role played each study skill one time, or Condition III, in which no modeling or role playing occurred, Condition I trainees met for two Structured Learning sessions for each of the two study skills, and role played each skill three times.

Figure 5. Experimental Design of Fischman (1985) Investigation

I	II	III
Structured Learning plus Transfer Enhancement	Structured Learning	Attention Control

2. *Stimulus Variability.* Condition I trainees, when role play-ing each study skill, did so each time with a different co-actor. In addi-tion, for the role plays conducted in the trainee's home (see number 3), two different stimulus situations per skill were utilized.

3. *Identical Elements.* For each study skill, the parent aide working with Condition I trainees presented to the parent *at home* one or more skill-relevant stimulus situations usually involving the parent's own child. The aide coached the parent regarding the skill behavioral steps to be used in these homework assignments, observed its in vivo application, and provided appropriate feedback.

4. *Programmed Reinforcement.* Parent aides were instructed to actively look for and energetically praise correct use of the study skills by Condition I parents after either the contrived role plays at home or following natural occurrences of correct skill usage.

The primary hypothesis in this investigation was that the com-bination of Structured Learning plus transfer enhancers would yield skill transfer (and perhaps even acquisition) effects superior to those obtained by either Structured Learning alone or by the attention con-trol procedures. Study results very strongly support this prediction. Analyses of variance yielded significant F values for both study skills on all study measures. Concretely, 1×3 analyses of variance across the three study conditions yielded significant outcomes for Using Self-control and Empathy, respectively, on the Direct Test ($F_{SC} = 25.30, p < .001; F_E = 27.00, p < .001$), Minimal Generalization Test ($F_{SC} = 6.44, p < .05; F_E = 3.78, p < .05$), Extended Generalization Test$_1$, that is, Parent Aide Rating Scale ratings of in-home use of skill ($F_{SC} = 59.49, p < .001; F_E = 51.87, p < .001$), Extended Generaliza-tion Test$_2$, that is, Parent Aide Rating Scale ratings of changes in pre-senting problems at home ($F = 68.72, p < .001$), and Extended Generalization Test$_3$, that is, live, challenging role play situations rel-evant to the two study skills presented to all trainees by the examiner ($F_{SC} = 15.89, p < .01; F_E = 14.06, p < .01$). Almost without excep-tion, post hoc Tukey tests following these significant overall compar-isons revealed, as predicted, significantly greater skill competence for Structured Learning plus transfer enhancers than for either Struc-tured Learning alone or attention control.

These four investigations combine to yield two rather clear con-clusions. First, Structured Learning has been shown across all four studies to be an effective means of teaching prosocial skill alterna-tives to aggression to trainees identified as abusive parents. Second, while Structured Learning alone fails to yield consistent extended (to the home) skill transfer effects, such effects are obtained when a series of techniques designed for transfer-enhancement purposes are employed in combination with Structured Learning. Since essentially all psychological and psychoeducational interventions suffer from a weakness or absence of transfer effects (Goldstein & Kanfer, 1979; Karoly & Steffen, 1980), this last conclusion is an especially important one for guiding future intervention efforts with either abusive parents or similar hard-to-change individuals.

References

Agras, W. S. (1967). Behavior therapy in the management of chronic schizophrenia. *American Journal of Psychiatry, 124,* 240–243.

Albee, G. W. (1980). Primary prevention and social problems. In G. Gerbner, C. J. Ross, & E. Zigler (Eds.), *Child abuse: An agenda for action.* New York: Oxford University Press.

Alexander, H. (1972). The social worker and the family. In C. H. Kempe & R. E. Helfer (Eds.), *Helping the battered child and his family.* Philadelphia: J. B. Lippincott.

Alfaro, J. D. (1978, March). *Summary report on the relationship between child abuse and neglect and later socially deviant behavior.* New York: New York State Assembly Select Committee on Child Abuse.

Almond, P. O. (1980). What we were up against: Media views of parents and children. In G. Gerbner, C. J. Ross, & E. Zigler (Eds.), *Child abuse: An agenda for action.* New York: Oxford University Press.

Alvy, K. T. (1975). Preventing child abuse. *American Psychologist, 30,* 921–928.

Ambrose, S., Hazzard, A., & Haworth, J. (1980). Cognitive-behavioral parenting groups for abusive parents. *Child Abuse and Neglect. 4,* 119–125.

American Humane Association. (1981). *The national study of child neglect and abuse reporting.* Denver, CO: American Humane Association.

Antler, S. (1978). Child abuse: An emerging social priority. *Social Work, 23,* 58–61.

Appelbaum, A. S. (1977). Developmental retardation in infants as a concomitant of physical child abuse. *Journal of Abnormal Child Psychology, 5,* 417–423.

Ayoub, C., & Pfeifer, D. R. (1977). An approach to primary prevention. The "At-Risk" program. *Children Today, 6,* 14–17.

Baer, A. M., & Wathey, R. B. (1977). Covert forms of child abuse: A preliminary study. *Child Psychiatry and Human Development, 8,* 115–128.

Bandura, A. (1969). *Principles of behavior modification.* New York: Holt, Rinehart & Winston.

Bandura, A. (1973). *Aggression: A social learning analysis.* Englewood Cliffs, NJ: Prentice-Hall.

Bandura, A. (1977). *Social learning theory.* Englewood Cliffs, NJ: Prentice-Hall.

Barahal, R. M., Waterman, J., & Martin, H. P. (1981). The social cognitive development of abused children. *Journal of Consulting and Clinical Psychology, 49,* 508–516.

Baron, M. A., Bejar, R. L., & Sheaff, P. J. (1970). Neurologic manifestations of the battered child syndrome. *Pediatrics, 45,* 1003–1007.

Beezley, P., Martin, H., & Alexander, H. (1976). Comprehensive family oriented therapy. In R. E. Helfer & C. H. Kempe (Eds.), *Child abuse and neglect: The family and the community.* Cambridge, MA: Ballinger.

Belsky, J. (1978). A theoretical analysis of child abuse remediation strategies. *Journal of Clinical Child Psychology, 7,* 117–121.

Bennie, E. H., & Sclare, A. B. (1969). The battered child syndrome. *American Journal of Psychiatry, 125,* 975–979.

Berlin, R. (1974). *Teaching acting-out adolescents prosocial conflict resolution through Structured Learning training of empathy.* Unpublished doctoral dissertation, Syracuse University, NY.

Billingsley, A. (1969). Family functioning in the low income black community. *Casework, 50,* 563–572.

Blager, F., & Martin, H. P. (1976). Speech and language of abused children. In H. P. Martin (Ed.), *The abused child: A multidisciplinary approach to developmental issues and treatment.* Cambridge, MA: Ballinger.

Blatt, B. (1980). The pariah industry: A diary from purgatory and other places. In G. Gerbner, C. J. Ross, & E. Zigler (Eds.), *Child abuse: An agenda for action.* New York: Oxford University Press.

Bryan, J. H., & Test, M. A. (1967). Models and helping: Naturalistic studies in aiding behavior. *Journal of Personality and Social Psychology, 6,* 400–407.

Buchanan, A., & Oliver, J. E. (1977). Abuse and neglect and a cause of mental retardation: A study of 140 children admitted to subnormality hospitals in Wiltshire. *British Journal of Psychiatry, 131,* 458–467.

Burgess, R. L. (1979). Child abuse: A social interactional analysis. In B. B. Lahey & A. E. Kazdin (Eds.), *Advances in clinical child psychology* (Vol. 2). New York: Plenum.

Burgess, R. L., Anderson, E. A., Shellenbach, E. A., & Conger, R. D. (1981). A social interactional approach to the study of abusive families. In *Advances in family intervention: Assessment and theory* (Vol. 2). Greenwich, CN: JAI Press.

Burgess, R. L., & Conger, R. D. (1978). Family interaction in abusive, neglectful, and normal families. *Child Development, 49,* 1163–1173.

Caffey, J. (1972). On the theory and practice of shaking infants. *American Journal of Diseases of Children, 124,* 161–169.

Callantine, M. F., & Warren, J. M. (1955). Learning sets in human concept formation. *Psychological Reports, 1,* 363–367.

Campbell, R. V., O'Brien, S., Bickett, A. D., & Lutzker, J. R. (1983). In-home parent training, treatment of migraine headaches and marital counseling as an ecobehavioral approach to prevent child abuse. *Journal of Behavior Therapy and Experimental Psychiatry, 14,* 147–154.

Carroll, J., Schaffer, C., Spensley, J., & Abramowitz, S. I. (1980). Family experiences of self-mutilating patients. *American Journal of Psychiatry, 137,* 852–853.

Christopherson, E. R., Kuehn, B. S., Grinstead, J. B., Barnard, J. D., Rainey, S. K., & Kuehn, F. E. (1976). A family training program for abuse and neglect families. *Journal of Pediatric Psychology, 1,* 90–94.

Cicchetti, D., Taraldson, B., & Egeland, B. (1978). Perspectives in the treatment and understanding of child abuse. In A. P. Goldstein (Ed.), *Prescriptions of child mental health and education.* New York: Pergamon Press.

Cohen, S. J., & Sussman, A. (1975). The incidence of child abuse in the United States. *Child Welfare, 54,* 432–443.

Conger, R. D. (1982). Behavioral intervention for child abuse. *The Behavior Therapist, 5,* 49–53.

Conger, R. D., Burgess, R. L., & Barrett, C. (1979). Child abuse related to life change and perceptions of illness: Some preliminary findings. *Family Coordinator, 28,* 73–78.

Conger, R. D., Lahey, B. B., & Smith, S. S. (1981). *An intervention program for child abuse: Modifying maternal depression and behavior.* Paper presented at Family Violence Research Conference, University of New Hampshire, Durham.

Crozier, J., & Katz, R. C. (1979). Social learning treatment of child abuse. *Journal of Behavior Therapy and Experimental Psychiatry, 10,* 213–220.

Culbertson, F. M. (1957). Modification of an emotionally held attitude through role playing. *Journal of Abnormal and Social Psychology, 54,* 230–233.

Daly, M., & Wilson, M. (1980). Discriminative parental solicitude: A biological perspective. *Journal of Marriage and the Family, 42,* 277–288.

DeBortali-Tregerthan, G. J. (1979). A behavioral treatment of child abuse: A case report. *Child Behavior Therapy, 1,* 287–293.

Delissovoy, V. (1973). Child care by adolescent parents. *Children Today, 2,* 22–25.

Delsordo, J. D. (1973). Protective casework for abused children. *Children, 10,* 213–218.

Denicola, J., & Sandler, J. (1980). Training abusive parents in child management and self-control skills. *Behavior Therapy, 11,* 263–270.

Dietrich, K. N., Starr, R. H., & Kaplan, M. G. (1980). Maternal stimulation and care of abused infants. In T. M. Field, S. Goldberg, D. Stern, & A. M. Sostek (Eds.), *High-risk infants and children.* New York: Academic Press.

Disbrow, M. A., Doerr, H., & Caulfield, C. (1977). Measuring the components of parents' potential for child abuse and neglect. *Child Abuse and Neglect, 1,* 279–296.

Dubanoski, R. A., Evans, I. M., & Higuchi, A. A. (1978). Analysis and treatment of child abuse: A set of behavioral propositions. *Child Abuse and Neglect, 2,* 153–172.

Duncan, C. P. (1958). Transfer after training with single versus multiple tasks. *Journal of Experimental Psychology, 55,* 63–72.

D'Zurilla, T. J., & Goldfried, M. R. (1971). Problem solving and behavior modification. *Journal of Abnormal Psychology, 78,* 107–126.

Ebbin, A. J., Gollub, M. H., Stein, A. M., & Wilson, M. G. (1969). Battered child syndrome at the Los Angeles County General Hospital. *American Journal of Diseases of Children, 118,* 660–667.

Egeland, B., & Brunnquell, D. (1979). An at-risk approach to the study of child abuse: Some preliminary findings. *Journal of the American Academy of Child Psychiatry, 18,* 219–235.

Egeland, B., & Sroufe, L. A. (1981a). Attachment and early maltreatment. *Child Development, 52,* 44–52.

Egeland, B., & Sroufe, L. A. (1981b). Developmental sequelae of maltreatment in infancy. *New Directions for Child Development, 11,* 77–92.

Ellis, H. (1965). *The transfer of learning.* New York: Macmillan.

Elmer, E. (1977). A follow-up study of traumatized children. *Pediatrics, 59,* 273–279.

Elmer, E. (1978). Effects of early neglect and abuse on latency age children. *Journal of Pediatric Psychology, 3,* 14–19.

Elmer, E., & Gregg, G. S. (1967). Developmental characteristics of abused children. *Journal of Pediatrics, 40,* 596–602.

Feindler, E. L., Marriott, S. A., & Iwata, M. (1984). Group anger control training for junior high school delinquents. *Cognitive Therapy and Research, 8,* 299–311.

Feshbach, N. D. (1980). Corporal punishment in the schools: Some paradoxes, some facts, some possible directions. In G. Gerbner, C. J. Ross, & E. Zigler (Eds.), *Child abuse: An agenda for action.* New York: Oxford University Press.

Feshbach, S. (1980). Child abuse and the dynamics of human aggression and violence. In G. Gerbner, C. J. Ross, & E. Zigler (Eds.), *Child abuse: An agenda for action.* New York: Oxford University Press.

Fischman, A. (1984). *Evaluating the effectiveness of Structured Learning with abusive parents.* Unpublished master's thesis, Syracuse University, NY.

Fischman, A. (1985). *The use of transfer enhancers in teaching self-control and empathy to abusive parents.* Unpublished doctoral dissertation, Syracuse University, NY.

Fitch, M. J., Cadol, R. V., Goldson, E., Wendell, T., Swartz, D., & Jackson, E. (1976). Cognitive development of abused and failure-to-thrive children. *Journal of Pediatric Psychology, 1,* 32–37.

Fontana, V. J. (1968). Further reflections on maltreatment of children. *New York Journal of Medicine, 68,* 2214–2215.

Fontana, V. J. (1971). *The maltreated child.* Springfield IL: Charles C. Thomas.

Frank, J. D. (1978). *Psychotherapy and the human predicament.* New York: Schocken Books.

Friedrich, W. M., & Boriskin, J. A. (1976). The role of the child in abuse: A review of the literature. *American Journal of Orthopsychiatry, 46,* 580–590.

Friedrich, W. M., & Boriskin, J. A. (1978). Primary prevention of child abuse: Focus on the special child. *Hospital and Community Psychiatry, 29,* 248–251.

Friedrich, W. N., & Einbender, A. J. (1983). The abused child: A psychological review. *Journal of Clinical Child Psychology, 12,* 244–256.

Friedrich, W. N., Einbender, A. J., & Luecke, W. J. (1983). Cognitive and behavioral characteristics of physically abused children. *Journal of Consulting and Clinical Psychology, 51,* 313–314.

Frude, N., & Goss, A. (1979). Parental anger: A general population survey. *Child Abuse and Neglect, 3,* 331–333.

Gaines, R., Sandgrund, A., Green, A. H., & Power, E. (1978). Etiological factors in child maltreatment: A multivariate study of abusing, neglecting, and normal mothers. *Journal of Abnormal Psychology, 87,* 531–540.

Gambrill, E. D. (1983). Behavioral intervention with child abuse and neglect. In M. Hersen, R. M. Eisler, & P. M. Miller (Eds.), *Progress in behavior modification* (Vol. 15). New York: Academic.

Garbarino, J. (1977). The human ecology of child maltreatment: A conceptual model for research. *Journal of Marriage and the Family, 39,* 721–735.

Garbarino, J., Crouter, A. C., & Sherman, D. (1977). Screening neighborhoods for intervention: A research model for child protective services. *Journal of Social Service Research, 1,* 135–145.

Gaylord, J. J. (1975). Wife battering: A preliminary survey of 100 cases. *British Journal of Medicine, 1,* 194–197.

Gelles, R. J. (1973). Child abuse as psychopathology: A sociological critique and reformation. *American Journal of Orthopsychiatry, 43,* 611–621.

Gelles, R. J. (1975). The social construction of child abuse. *American Journal of Orthopsychiatry, 45,* 363–371.

Gelles, R. J. (1978). Violence toward children in the United States. *American Journal of Orthopsychiatry, 48,* 580–592.

Gelles, R. J. (1980a). A profile of violence toward children in the United States. In G. Gerbner, C. J. Ross, & E. Zigler (Eds.), *Child abuse: An agenda for action*. New York: Oxford University Press.

Gelles, R. J. (1980b). Violence in the family: A review of research in the seventies. *Journal of Marriage and the Family, 42*, 873–885.

Gelles, R. J. (1982a). An exchange/social control approach to understanding intrafamily violence. *The Behavior Therapist, 5*, 5–8.

Gelles, R. J. (1982b). Problems in defining and labeling child abuse. In R. H. Starr (Ed.), *Child abuse prediction: Policy implications*. Cambridge, MA: Ballinger.

Gelles, R. J., & Straus, M. A. (1979). Determinants of violence in the family: Toward a theoretical integration. In W. R. Burr, R. Hill, F. I. Nye, & I. L. Reiss (Eds.), *Contemporary theories about the family*. New York: Free Press.

Gerbner, G. (1980). Children and power on television: The other side of the picture. In G. Gerbner, C. J. Ross, & E. Zigler (Eds.), *Child abuse: An agenda for action*. New York: Oxford University Press.

Gil, D. C. (1970). *Violence against children: Physical child abuse in the United States*. Cambridge, MA: Harvard University Press.

Gilbert, M. T. (1976). Behavioral approach to the treatment of child abuse. *Nursing Times, 72*, 140–143.

Giovannoni, J. M., & Billingsley, A. (1970). Child neglect among the poor: A study of parental adequacy in families of three ethnic groups. *Child Welfare, 49*, 196–204.

Gittelman, M. (1965). Behavior rehearsal as a technique of child treatment. *Journal of Child Psychology and Psychiatry, 6*, 251–255.

Goldfried, M. R., & Trier, C. A. (1974). Effectiveness of relaxation as an active coping skill. *Journal of Abnormal Psychology, 83*, 348–355.

Goldstein, A. P. (1973). *Structured learning therapy: Toward a psychotherapy for the poor*. New York: Academic Press.

Goldstein, A. P. (Ed.). (1978). *Prescriptions for child mental health and education*. New York: Pergamon Press.

Goldstein, A. P. (1981). *Psychological skill training: The Structured Learning technique*. New York: Pergamon Press.

Goldstein, A. P. (1983). Behavior modification approaches to aggression prevention. In Center for Research on Aggression (Ed.), *Prevention and control of aggression*. New York: Pergamon Press.

Goldstein, A. P., Glick, B., Zimmerman, D., Reiner, S., Coultry, T. A., & Gold, D. (in press). Aggression replacement training: A comprehensive intervention for the acting-out delinquent. *Journal of Correctional Education*.

Goldstein, A. P., & Goodhart, A. (1973). The use of structured learning for empathy-enhancement in paraprofessional psychotherapist training. *Journal of Community Psychology, 1*, 168–173.

Goldstein, A. P., & Kanfer, F. (Eds.). (1979). *Maximizing treatment gains.* New York: Academic Press.

Goldstein, A. P., Monti, P. J., Sardino, T. J., & Green, D. J. (1977). *Police crisis intervention.* New York: Pergamon Press.

Goldstein, A. P., & Rosenbaum, A. (1982). *Agress-Less.* Englewood Cliffs, NJ: Prentice-Hall.

Goldstein, A. P., & Sorcher, M. (1973, March). Changing managerial behavior by applied learning techniques. *Training and Development Journal, 36*–39.

Goldstein, A. P., & Sorcher, M. (1974). *Changing supervisor behavior.* New York: Pergamon Press.

Goldstein, A. P., Sprafkin, R. P., & Gershaw, N. J. (1976). *Skill training for community living: Applying structured learning therapy.* New York: Pergamon Press.

Goldstein, A. P., Sprafkin, R. P., Gershaw, N. J., & Klein, P. (1980). *Skillstreaming the adolescent.* Champaign, IL: Research Press.

Goldstein, A. P., & Stein, N. (1976). *Prescriptive psychotherapies.* New York: Pergamon Press.

Gottlieb, B. H. (1980). The role of individual and social support in preventing maltreatment. In J. Garbarino & S. H. Stocking (Eds.), *Protecting children from abuse and neglect.* San Francisco: Jossey-Bass.

Gray, J., Cutler, C., Dean, J., & Kempe, C. H. (1976). Perinatal assessment of mother-baby interaction. In R. E. Helfer & C. J. Kempe (Eds.), *Child abuse and neglect: The family and the community.* Cambridge, MA: Ballinger.

Green, A. H. (1978a). Psychopathology of abused children. *Journal of the American Academy of Child Psychiatry, 17,* 92–103.

Green, A. H. (1978b). Self-destructive behavior in battered children. *American Journal of Psychiatry, 135,* 579–582.

Green, A., Gaines, R. W., & Sandgrund, A. (1974). Child abuse: Pathological syndrome of family interaction. *American Journal of Psychiatry, 131,* 882–886.

Green, A. H., Voeller, K., Gaines, R. W., & Kubie, J. (1981). Neurological impairment in maltreated children. *Child Abuse and Neglect, 5,* 129–134.

Greenleaf, D. (1978). *The use of programmed transfer of training and Structured Learning therapy with disruptive adolescents in a school setting.* Unpublished master's thesis, Syracuse University, NY.

Gregg, G., & Elmer, E. (1969). Infant injuries: Accident or abuse? *Pediatrics, 44,* 434–439.

Gruber, R. P. (1971). Behavior therapy: Problems in generalization. *Behavior Therapy, 2,* 361–368.

Halperin, S. L. (1981). Abused and non-abused children's perceptions of their mothers, fathers and siblings: Implications for a comprehensive family treatment plan. *Family Relations, 30,* 89–96.

Heiko, R. (1980). *Consultee-centered and problem-solving consultation services to paraprofessionals working with child abusing parents in Structured Learning Therapy program.* Unpublished doctoral dissertation, Syracuse University, NY.

Helfer, R. E. (1973). The etiology of child abuse. *Pediatrics, 51,* 777–779.

Helfer, R. E. (1978). Introduction: Putting child abuse and neglect into perspective. In B. J. Kalisch (Ed.), *Child abuse and neglect: An annotated bibliography.* Westport, CT: Greenwood.

Helfer, R. E., & Kempe, C. H. (Eds.).(1976). *Child abuse and neglect: The family and the community.* Cambridge, MA: Ballinger.

Hellsten, P., & Katila, O. (1965). Murder and other homicides by children under 15 in Finland. *Psychiatric Quarterly, 38,* 54–74.

Herrenkohl, E. C., & Herrenkohl, R. C. (1979). A comparison of abused children and their nonabused siblings. *Journal of the American Academy of Child Psychiatry, 18,* 260–269.

Herrenkohl, R. C., Herrenkohl, E. C., Egolf, B., & Seech, M. (1979). The repetition of child abuse: How frequently does it occur. *International Journal of Child Abuse and Neglect, 3,* 67–72.

Hughes, R. C. (1974). A clinic's parent-performance training program for child abusers. *Hospital and Community Psychiatry, 25,* 779–782.

Hummel, J. (1979). *Session variability and skill content as transfer enhancers in Structured Learning training.* Unpublished doctoral dissertation, Syracuse University, NY.

Hunter, R. S., & Kilstrom, N. (1979). Breaking the cycle in abusive families. *American Journal of Psychiatry, 136,* 1320–1322.

Hunter, R., Kilstrom, N., Kraybill, E., & Loda, F. (1978). Antecedents of child abuse and neglect in premature infants: A prospective study in a newborn intensive care unit. *Pediatrics, 6,* 629–635.

Hyman, C. A. (1978). Some characteristics of abusing families referred to the NSPCC. *British Journal of Social Work, 8,* 171–179.

Hyman, C. A., & Mitchell, R. (1975). A psychological study of child battering. *Health Visitor, 38,* 294–296.

Isaacs, C. D. (1981). A brief review of the characteristics of abuse-prone parents. *The Behavior Therapist, 4,* 5–8.

Isaacs, C. D. (1982). Treatment of child abuse: A review of the behavioral interventions. *Journal of Applied Behavior Analysis, 15,* 273–294.

Jeffery, M. (1976). Practical ways to change parent-child interaction in families of children at risk. In R. E. Helfer & S. H. Kempe (Eds.), *Child abuse and neglect: The family and the community.* Cambridge, MA: Ballinger.

Jensen, R. E. (1976). A behavior modification program to remediate child abuse. *Journal of Clinical Child Psychology, 5,* 30–32.

Johnson, B., & Morse, H. A. (1968). Injured children and their parents. *Children, 15,* 147–152.

Justice, B., & Duncan, D. F. (1976). Life crisis as a precursor to child abuse. *Public Health Reports, 91,* 110–115.

Justice, B., & Justice, R. (1976). *The abusing family.* New York: Human Sciences.

Kahn, A. J., & Kamerman, S. B. (1980). Child abuse: A comparative perspective. In G. Gerbner, C. J. Ross, & E. Zigler (Eds.), *Child abuse: An agenda for action.* New York: Oxford University Press.

Karoly, P., & Steffen, J. (1980). *Improving the long term effects of psychotherapy.* New York: Gardner Press.

Kazdin, A. E., & Wilcoxon, L. A. (1976). Systematic desensitization and nonspecific treatment effects: A methodological evaluation. *Psychological Bulletin, 83,* 729–758.

Keller, H. R., & Erné, D. (1983). Child abuse: Toward a comprehensive model. In Center for Research Aggression, *Prevention and control of aggression.* New York: Pergamon Press.

Kempe, C. H., & Helfer, R. E. (Eds.). (1972). *Helping the battered child and his family.* Philadelphia: J. B. Lippincott.

Kempe, R., & Kempe, C. H. (1976). *Child abuse and neglect: The family and the community.* Cambridge, MA: Ballinger.

Kempe, C. H., Silverman, F. N., Steele, B. F., Droegenmueller, W., & Silver, H. K. (1962). The battered child syndrome. *Journal of the American Medical Association, 181,* 17–24.

Kimball, W. H., Stewart, R. B., Conger, R. D., & Burgess, R. L. (1980). A comparison of family interaction in single- versus two-parent abusive, neglectful, and control families. In T. Field (Ed.), *High-risk infants and children.* New York: Academic Press.

Kinard, E. M. (1980). Emotional development in physically abused children. *American Journal of Orthopsychiatry, 50,* 686–696.

Kinard, E. M. (1982). Experiencing child abuse: Effects on emotional adjustment. *American Journal of Orthopsychiatry, 52,* 82–91.

King, B. T., & Janis, I. L. (1956). Comparison of the effectiveness of improvised vs. non-improvised role playing in producing opinion changes. *Human Relations, 9,* 177–186.

Kline, D. F. (1977). Educational and psychological problems of abused children. *International Journal of Child Abuse and Neglect, 1,* 301–307.

Korbin, J. (1977). Anthropological contributions to the study of child abuse. *Child Abuse and Neglect, 1,* 7–24.

Koski, M. A., & Ingram, E. M. (1977). Child abuse and neglect: Effects on Bayley Scale Scores. *Journal of Abnormal Child Psychology, 5,* 79–91.

Krumboltz, J. D., & Schroeder, W. W. (1965). Promoting career planning through reinforcement. *Personnel and Guidance Journal, 44,* 19–26.

Lack, D. Z. (1975). *Problem-solving training, Structured Learning training, and didactic instruction in the preparation of paraprofessional mental health personnel for the utilization of contingency management techniques.* Unpublished doctoral dissertation, Syracuse University, NY.

Lang, P. (1968). Fear reduction and fear behavior problems in treating a construct. In J. M. Shlien (Ed.), *Research in psychotherapy* (Vol. 3). Washington, DC: American Psychological Association.

Lauer, B., Broeck, E., & Grossman, M. (1974). Battered child syndrome: Review of 130 patients with controls. *Pediatrics, 54,* 67–70.

Lewis, D. O., Shanok, S. S., Pincus, J. H., & Glaser, G. H. (1979). Violent juvenile delinquents. *Journal of the American Academy of Child Psychiatry, 18,* 307–319.

Liberman, B. (1970). *The effect of modeling procedures on attraction and disclosure in a psychotherapy analogue.* Unpublished doctoral dissertation, Syracuse University, NY.

Light, R. (1973). Abused and neglected children in America: A study of alternative policies. *Harvard Educational Review, 43,* 556–598.

Litwack, S. E. (1976). *The use of the helper therapy principle to increase therapeutic effectiveness and reduce therapeutic resistance: Structured Learning therapy with resistant adolescents.* Unpublished doctoral dissertation, Syracuse University, NY.

Lopez, M. (1977). *The effects of overlearning and prestructuring in Structured Learning therapy with geriatric patients.* Unpublished doctoral dissertation, Syracuse University, NY.

Lopez, M. A., Hoyer, W. J., Goldstein, A. P., Gershaw, N. J., & Sprafkin, R. P. (1980). Effects on overlearning and incentive on the acquisition and transfer of interpersonal skills with institutionalized elderly. *Journal of Gerontology, 35,* 403–408.

Lukianowicz, N. (1971). Battered children. *Psychiatrica Clinica, 4,* 257–280.

Lutzker, J. R. (1983). Project 12-Ways: Treating child abuse and neglect from an ecobehavioral perspective. In R. F. Dangel & R. A. Polster (Eds.), *Parent training: Foundations of research and practice.* New York: Guilford.

Lutzker, J. R., Frame, R. E., & Rice, J. M. (1982). Project 12-Ways: An ecobehavioral approach to the treatment and prevention of child abuse and neglect. *Education and Treatment of Children, 5,* 141–155.

Lynch, M. A. (1975). Ill-health and child abuse. *The Lancet,* 317–319.

Lynch, M. A. (1978). The prognosis of child abuse. *Journal of Child Psychology and Psychiatry, 19,* 175–180.

Lystad, M. H. (1975). Violence at home: A review of the literature. *American Journal of Orthopsychiatry, 45,* 328–345.

MacKeith, R. (1975). Speculations on some possible long-term effects. In A. W. Franklin (Ed.), *Concerning child abuse.* New York: Churchill Livingstone.

Maden, M. F., & Wrench, D. F. (1977). Significant findings in child abuse research. *Victimology, 2,* 196–224.

Martin, H. P. (1972). The child and his development. In C. H. Kempe & R. E. Helfer (Eds.), *Helping the battered child and his family.* Philadelphia: J. B. Lippincott.

Martin, H. P., & Beezley, P. (1976). Personality of abused children. In H. P. Martin (Ed.), *The abused child: A multidisciplinary approach to developmental issues and treatment.* Cambridge, MA: Ballinger.

Martin, H. P., & Beezley, P. (1977). Behavioral observations of abused children. *Developmental Medicine and Clinical Neurology, 19,* 373–387.

Martin, H. P., Beezley, P., Conway, E., & Kempe, C. H. (1974). The development of abused children. *Advances in Pediatrics, 21,* 25–73.

McGinnis, E., & Goldstein, A. P. (1984). *Skillstreaming the elementary school child.* Champaign, IL: Research Press.

Melnick, B., & Hurley, J. R. (1969). Distinctive personality attributes of child-abusing mothers. *Journal of Consulting and Clinical Psychology, 33,* 746–749.

Merrill, E. J. (1962). Physical abuse of children: An agency study. In *Protecting the battered child.* Denver: Children's Division, The American Humane Association.

Milner, J. S., & Wimberley, R. C. (1979). An inventory for the identification of child abuse. *Journal of Clinical Psychology, 35,* 95–100.

Milner, J. S., & Wimberly, R. C. (1980). Prediction and explanation of child abuse. *Journal of Clinical Psychology, 36,* 875–884.

Mirandy, J. (1976). Preschool for abused children. In H. P. Martin (Ed.), *The abused child: A multidisciplinary approach to developmental issues and treatment.* Cambridge, MA: Ballinger.

Moore, J. G. (1975). Yo-yo children-victims of matrimonial violence. *Child Welfare, 54,* 557–566.

Morse, C. W., Sahler, O. J., & Friedman, S. B. (1970). A three-year follow-up study of abused and neglected children. *American Journal of Diseases of Children, 120,* 439–446.

Newberger, E. H., & Bourne, R. (1978). The medicalization and legalization of child abuse. *American Journal of Orthopsychiatry, 48,* 593–607.

Novaco, R. W. (1975). *Anger control.* Lexington, MA: Lexington Books.

Oliver, J. E. (1975). Microcephaly following baby battering and shaking. *British Medical Journal, 2,* 262–264.

Oliver, J. E., & Taylor, A. (1971). Five generations of ill-treated children in one family pedigree. *British Journal of Psychiatry, 119,* 473–480.

Orenstein, R. (1973). *Effect of teaching patients to focus on their feelings on level of experiencing a subsequent interview.* Unpublished doctoral dissertation, Syracuse University, NY.

Osgood, C. E. (1953). *Method and theory in experimental psychology.* New York: Oxford University Press.

Ounsted, C., Oppenheimer, R., & Lindsay, J. (1975). The psychopathology and psychotherapy of the families: Aspects of bonding failure. In A. W. Franklin (Ed.), *Concerning child abuse.* New York: Churchill Livingstone.

Parke, R. D., & Collmer, C. W. (1975). Child abuse: An interdisciplinary analysis. In E. M. Hetherington (Ed.), *Review of child development research* (Vol. 5). Chicago: University of Chicago.

Patterson, G. R. (1974). Intervention for boys with conduct problems: Multiple settings, treatment, and criteria. *Journal of Consulting and Clinical Psychology, 42,* 471–481.

Patterson, G. R. (1982). *Coercive family process.* Eugene, OR: Castalia.

Patterson, G. R., & Anderson, D. (1964). Peers as social reinforcers. *Child Development, 35,* 951–960.

Patterson, G. R., & Cobb, J. A. (1971). A dyadic analysis of "aggressive" behavior. In J. P. Hill (Ed.), *Minnesota symposia on child psychology* (Vol. 5). Minneapolis: University of Minnesota Press.

Patterson, G. R., & Cobb, J. A. (1973). Stimulus control for classes of noxious behavior. In J. S. Knutson (Ed.), *The control of aggression: Implications from basic research.* Chicago: Aldine.

Patterson, G. R., & Reid, J. B. (1970). Reciprocity and coercion: Two facets of social systems. In C. Newunger & J. Michael (Eds.), *Behavior modification in clinical psychology.* New York: Appleton-Century-Crofts.

Pelton, L. H. (1978). Child abuse and neglect: The myth of classlessness. *American Journal of Orthopsychiatry, 48,* 608–617.

Pelton, L. H. (1979). Interpreting family violence data. *American Journal of Orthopsychiatry, 49,* 194.

Perry, M. A., Doran, L. D., & Wells, E. A. (1983). Developmental and behavioral characteristics of the physically abused child. *Journal of Clinical Child Psychology, 12,* 320–324.

Pfeifer, D. R., & Ayoub, C. (1976). An approach to the prophylaxis of child abuse and neglect. *Journal of the Oklahoma State Medical Association, 69,* 162–167.

Polokow, R. L., & Peabody, D. B. (1975). Behavioral treatment of child abuse. *International Journal of Offender Therapy and Comparative Criminology, 19,* 100–103.

Reaveley, W., & Gilbert, M. T. (1976). The behavioral approach to potential child abuse—two illustrative case reports. *Social Work Today, 7,* 166–168.

Reaveley, W., & Gilbert, M. T. (1979). The analysis and treatment of child abuse by behavioural psychotherapy. *Child Abuse and Neglect, 3,* 509–514.

Reid, J. B., Taplin, P. S., & Lorber, R. (1981). A social interactional approach to the treatment of abusive families. In R. B. Stuart (Ed.), *Violent behavior: Social learning approaches to prediction, management and treatment.* New York: Brunner/Mazel.

Reidy, T. J. (1977). The aggressive characteristics of abused and neglected children. *Journal of Clinical Psychology, 33,* 1140–1145.

Rimm, D. C., & Masters, J. C. (1979). *Behavior therapy: Techniques and empirical findings.* New York: Academic Press.

Robinson, R. (1973). *Evaluation of a Structured Learning empathy training program for lower socioeconomic status home-aide trainees.* Unpublished master's thesis, Syracuse University, NY.

Rose, E., & Hardman, M. L. (1981). The abused mentally retarded child. *Education and Training of the Mentally Retarded, 16,* 114–118.

Ross, C. J. (1980). The lessons of the past: Defining and controlling child abuse in the United States. In G. Gerbner, C. J. Ross, & E. Zigler (Eds.), *Child abuse: An agenda for action.* New York: Oxford University Press.

Ross, C. J., & Zigler, E. (1980). An agenda for action. In G. Gerbner, C. J. Ross, & E. Zigler (Eds.), *Child abuse: An agenda for action.* New York: Oxford University Press.

Sadler, O. W., & Seyden, T. (1976). Groups for parents: A guide for teaching child management to parents. *Journal of Community Psychology, 4,* 3–63.

Sameroff, A. J., & Chandler, M. J. (1975). Reproductive risk and the continuum of caretaking casualty. In F. D. Horowitz (Ed.), *Review of child development research* (Vol. 4). Chicago: University of Chicago Press.

Sandford, D. A., & Tustin, R. D. (1974). Behavioural treatment of parental assault on a child. *New Zealand Psychologist, 2,* 76–82.

Sandgrund, A., Gaines, R. W., & Green, A. H. (1974). Child abuse and mental retardation: A problem of cause and effect. *American Journal of Mental Deficiency, 79,* 327–330.

Sandler, J., Van Dercar, C., & Milhoan, M. (1978). Training child abusers in the use of positive reinforcement practices. *Behavior Research and Therapy, 16,* 169–175.

Savino, A. B., & Sanders, R. W. (1973). Working with abusive parents: Group therapy and home visits. *American Journal of Nursing, 73,* 482–484.

Schneider, C., Helfer, R. E., & Pollock, C. (1972). The predictive questionnaire: A preliminary report. In C. H. Kempe & R. E. Helfer (Eds.), *Helping the battered child and his family.* Philadelphia: J. B. Lippincott.

Schneider, C., Hoffmeister, J. K., & Helfer, R. E. (1976). A predictive screening questionnaire for potential problems in mother-child interaction. In R. E. Helfer & C. H. Kempe (Eds.), *Child abuse and neglect: The family and the community.* Cambridge, MA: Ballinger.

Schneider, C., Pollock, C., & Helfer, R. E. (1972). Interviewing the parents. In C. H. Kempe & R. E. Helfer (Eds.), *Helping the battered child and his family.* Philadelphia: J. B. Lippincott.

Schneiman, R. (1972). *An evaluation of Structured Learning and didactic learning as methods of training behavior modification skills to lower and middle socioeconomic level teacher-aides.* Unpublished doctoral dissertation, Syracuse University, NY.

Sherrod, K. B., O'Connor, S., Vietze, P. M., & Altemeier, W. A. (1984). Child health and maltreatment. *Child Development, 55,* 1174–1183.

Shore, E., & Sechrest, L. (1961). Concept attainment as a function of number of positive instances presented. *Journal of Educational Psychology, 52,* 303–307.

Signorielli, N. (1980). Covering abuse: Content and policy—magazine coverage. In G. Gerbner, C. J. Ross, & E. Zigler (Eds.), *Child abuse: An agenda for action.* New York: Oxford University Press.

Silver, L. B., Dublin, C., & Lourie, R. (1969). Does violence breed violence? Contributions from a study of the child abuse syndrome. *American Journal of Psychiatry, 126,* 404–407.

Simons, B., Downs, E. F., Hurster, M. M., & Archer, M. (1966). Child abuse: Epidemiologic study of medically reported cases. *New York State Journal of Medicine, 66,* 2783–2788.

Smith, J. E. (1984). Non-accidental injury to children—I: A review of behavioural interventions. *Behaviour Research and Therapy, 22,* 331–347.

Smith, J. E., & Rachman, S. J. (1984). Non-accidental injury to children—II: A controlled evaluation of a behavioural management programme. *Behaviour Research and Therapy, 22,* 349–366.

Smith, J. E., Rachman, S. J., & Yule, B. (1984). Non-accidental injury to children—III: Methodological problems of evaluative treatment research. *Behaviour Research and Therapy, 22,* 367–383.

Smith, S. M., & Hanson, R. (1974). 134 battered children: A medical and psychological study. *British Medical Journal, 3,* 666–670.

Smith, S. M., & Hanson, R. (1975). Interpersonal relationships and child-rearing practices in 214 parents of battered children. *British Journal of Psychiatry, 127,* 513–525.

Smith, S. M., Hanson, R., & Noble, S. (1975). Parents of battered children: A controlled study. In A. W. Franklin (Ed.), *Concerning child abuse.* New York: Churchill Livingstone.

Solomon, E. J. (1977). *Mastery induction and helper structuring as transfer-enhancers in teaching self-control to abusive parents.* Unpublished doctoral dissertation, Syracuse University, NY.

Spinetta, J. J., & Rigler, D. (1972). The child-abusing parent: A psychological review. *Psychological Bulletin, 77,* 296–304.

Starr, R. H. (1982). A research-based approach to the prediction of child abuse. In R. H. Starr (Ed.), *Child abuse prediction: Policy implications.* Cambridge, MA: Ballinger.

Steele, B. F. (1975). Working with abusive parents from a psychiatric point of view. *Children Today, 4,* 3–5.

Steele, B. F. (1976a). Experience with an inter-disciplinary concept. In R. E. Helfer & C. H. Kempe (Eds.), *Child abuse and neglect: The family and the community.* Cambridge, MA: Ballinger.

Steele, B. F. (1976b). Violence within the family. In R. E. Helfer & C. H. Kempe (Eds.), *Child abuse and neglect: The family and the community.* Cambridge, MA: Ballinger.

Steele, B. F., & Pollock, C. B. (1968). A psychiatric study of parents who abuse infants and small children. In R. E. Helfer & C. H. Kempe (Eds.), *The battered child.* Chicago: University of Chicago Press.

Stein, T. J., & Gambrill, E. D. (1976). Behavioral techniques in foster care. *Social Work, 21,* 34–39.

Stein, T. J., Gambrill, E. D., & Wiltse, K. T. (1978). *Children in foster homes: Achieving continuity of care.* New York: Praeger.

Steinberg, L. D., Catalano, R., & Dooley, D. (1981). Economic antecedents of child abuse and neglect. *Child Development, 52,* 975–985.

Steinmetz, S., & Straus, M. (1974). *Violence in the family.* New York: Dodd, Mead.

Straker, G., & Jacobson, R. S. (1981). Aggression, emotional maladjustment, and empathy in the abused child. *Developmental Psychology, 17,* 762–765.

Straus, M. A. (1979a). Family patterns and child abuse in a nationally representative American sample. *Child Abuse and Neglect, 3,* 213–225.

Straus, M. A. (1979b). Measuring intrafamily conflict and violence: The Conflict Tactics (CT) scales. *Journal of Marriage and the Family, 41,* 75–88.

Sutton-Simon, K. (1973). *The effects of two types of modeling and rehearsal procedures upon the adequacy of social behavior of hospitalized schizophrenics.* Unpublished doctoral dissertation, Syracuse University, NY.

Swanstrom, C. R. (1974). *An examination of Structured Learning therapy and the helper therapy principle in teaching a self-control strategy in school children with conduct problems.* Unpublished doctoral dissertation, Syracuse University, NY.

Tharp, R. G., & Wetzel, R. J. (1969). *Behavior modification in the natural environment.* New York: Academic Press.

Thomson, E. M., Paget, N. W., Bates, D. W., Mesch, M., & Putnam, T. I. (1971). *Child abuse: A community challenge.* East Aurora, NY: Henry Stewart.

Thorndike, E. L., & Woodworth, R. S. (1901). The influence of improvement in one mental function upon the efficiency of other functions. *Psychological Review, 8,* 247–261.

Tracy, J. J., Ballard, C. M., & Clark, E. H. (1975). Child abuse project: A followup. *Social Work, 20,* 398–399.

Tracy, J. J., & Clark, E. H. (ʼ1974). Treatment for child abusers. *Social Work, 19,* 338–342.

Trief, P. M. (1977). *The reduction of egocentrism in emotionally disturbed adolescents.* Unpublished doctoral dissertation, Syracuse University, NY.

Valins, S., & Ray, A. (1967). Effects of cognitive desensitization on avoidant behavior. *Journal of Personality and Social Psychology, 7,* 345–350.

Wahler, R. G. (1980). The insular mother: Her problems in parent child treatment. *Journal of Applied Behavior Analysis, 13,* 207–219.

Wasserman, G. A., Green, A., & Allen, R. (1983). Going beyond abuse: Maladaptive patterns of interaction in abusing mother-infant pairs. *Journal of the American Academy of Child Psychiatry, 22,* 245–252.

Wolfe, D. A., & Sandler, J. (1981). Training abusive parents in effective child management. *Behavior Modification, 5,* 320–335.

Wolfe, D. A., Sandler, J., & Kaufman, K. (1981). A competency-based parent training program for child abusers. *Journal of Consulting and Clinical Psychology, 49,* 633–640.

Wolfe, D. A., St. Lawrence, J., Graves, K., Brehony, K., Bradlyn, D., & Kelly, J. A. (1982). Intensive behavioral parent training for a child abusive parent. *Behavior Therapy, 13,* 438–451.

Wood, M. (1977). *Acquisition and transfer of assertiveness in passive and aggressive adolescents through the use of Structured Learning therapy.* Unpublished doctoral dissertation, Syracuse University, NY.

Young, L. (1964). *Wednesday's children: A study of child neglect and abuse.* New York: McGraw-Hill.

Zalba, S. R. (1966). The abused child: I. A survey of the problem. *Social Work, 11,* 3–16.

Zalba, S. R. (1967). The abused child: II. A typology for classification and treatment. *Social Work, 12,* 70–79.

Zigler, E. (1980). Controlling child abuse: Do we have the knowledge and/or the will? In G. Gerbner, C. J. Ross, & E. Zigler (Eds.), *Child abuse: An agenda for action.* New York: Oxford University Press.

Zuckerman, K., Ambuel, J., & Bandman, R. (1972). Child neglect and abuse: A study of cases evaluated at Columbia Children's Hospital in 1968–1969. *Ohio State Medical Journal, 68,* 629–632.

Index

About the Authors

Arnold P. Goldstein (Ph.D., Pennsylvania State, 1959) is Professor of Psychology and Director of the Center for Research on Aggression at Syracuse University. His career-long interest has been in developing and evaluating treatment approaches designed particularly for low-income clients. In 1970, he began building, applying, and experimentally testing Structured Learning, the psychoeducational skills training approach examined in the present book. Its wide applicability and effectiveness has been presented in such books by Goldstein and his colleagues as *Structured Learning Therapy: Toward a Psychotherapy for the Poor* (1973), *Skill Training for Community Living* (1976), *Skillstreaming the Adolescent* (1980), *Psychological Skill Training* (1981), and *Skillstreaming the Elementary School Child* (1984). Professor Goldstein's companion interest has been in aggression and aggression control, reflected in his books *In Response to Aggression* (1981), *Aggression in Global Perspective* (1983), *Prevention and Control of Aggression* (1983), *Aggress-Less* (1982), and *Youth Violence* (1985).

Harold R. Keller is Associate Professor of Psychology and Education at Syracuse University. He received his doctorate in 1968 from Florida State University and worked at the University of South Carolina before coming to Syracuse University in 1975. He is also the Director of the Syracuse University School Psychology Program and a member of the Center for Research on Aggression. His interests are in studying alternative assessment strategies with socioculturally different and handicapped children and in children's interactions with peers and adults (teachers, parents). In addition to journal articles on these topics, he has written book chapters on child abuse, behavioral assessment, and behavioral observation.

Diane Erné has been Executive Director of Alliance, a child and elder abuse coordination and parent aide program, since its

179

inception in 1972. Alliance runs one of the largest parent aide programs in the country and serves over 700 families annually. Ms. Erné has been involved in the development and marketing of a number of videotapes and training manuals dealing with coordination in child and elder abuse, parent aide training, and interviewing and treating the incestuous family. She was formerly a Child Protective Services worker with the Onondaga County Department of Social Services, Syracuse, New York, and later a supervisor within that department. She is an Associate Director of Catholic Charities of Syracuse, of which Alliance is a division.

Ms. Erné was a faculty member of the American Humane Association from 1981 to 1984 and is presently a faculty member of Action for Child Protection, a national training organization. She has been a lecturer and consultant throughout the United States and Canada and has done extensive training and curriculum development with Cornell University and the New York State Department of Social Services in law enforcement/protective joint intervention in child sexual abuse cases.

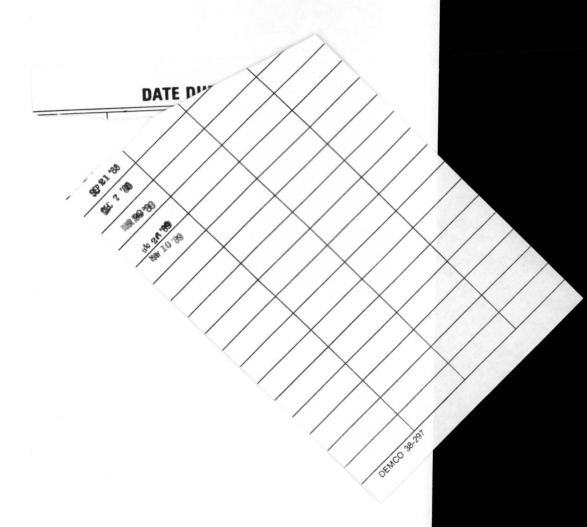